D0378554

the better world SHOPPING GUIDE

EVERY DOLLAR MAKES A DIFFERENCE

the better world SHOPPING GUIDE

Ellis Jones

new society PUBLISHERS

Copyright © 2017 by Ellis Jones. All rights reserved.

Cover concept by Ellis Jones. Design by Diane McIntosh.
Images: Getty Images/Photodisc Green.

Printed in Canada.

Paperback ISBN: 978-0-86571-862-3
eISBN: 978-1-55092-659-0

Inquiries regarding requests to reprint all or part of *The Better World Shopping Guide* should be addressed to New Society Publishers at the address below.

To order directly from the publishers, please call toll-free (North America) 1-800-567-6772, or order online at www.newsociety.com.

Any other inquiries can be directed by mail to
New Society Publishers
P.O. Box 189, Gabriola Island, BC V0R 1X0, Canada
1-800-567-6772

Cataloging in Publication Data:
A catalog record for this publication is available from the National Library of Canada.

Funded by the Government of Canada | Financé par le gouvernement du Canada | Canada

New Society Publishers' mission is to publish books that contribute in fundamental ways to building an ecologically sustainable and just society, and to do so with the least possible impact on the environment, in a manner that models this vision.

new society PUBLISHERS

Certified B Corporation

FSC www.fsc.org MIX Paper from responsible sources FSC® C016245

Contents

APPRECIATION

I am very grateful to Paul Todisco, Collin Ahrens, Mark Fairbrother, Tom McGlynn, Jason Logan, Brett Jacobs, J.P. Meyer, James Beam, Kristin Wallace, Jacob O'Brien, and Warren Zeger for their hard work testing the guide and researching brands in the real world; Greenley Littlejohn, Daniel Schulz-Jackson, and Charlie Marcotte for helping update the website; Daniel Newberger for helping me update many of my databases; and to my wife, Ara Francis, for her unwavering advocacy and dedication to getting this project the recognition and support it deserves. Also, a very special thank you to the good people at Free Range, Christie Communications, and Pachamama Alliance, who have been incredible in making important connections for me around this work.

I am also very grateful to you, the reader, for picking up this book. I'd like to say (because you may never hear it from anyone else) on behalf of all of the people on this planet whom you will never meet and all the natural places you will never see...

Thank you.

6TH EDITION NOTES

A decade after the 1st edition was published, I am humbled to think that this little book has sold nearly 150,000 copies.

In 2017, even more people are beginning to question the nature of our democracy and its relationship to our most powerful corporations and our wealthiest citizens. Given that our current US president is a billionaire and the Secretary of State is the former CEO of ExxonMobil (#1 on the Top 20 Worst List since the 1st edition), the connections between our economic and political power centers have become difficult to ignore.

To regenerate our own economic voice, we'll need some powerful tools. In this edition you'll find

✓ More than 2000 companies evaluated
✓ 75+ sources of reliable data cited
✓ New and Updated Top 10 & Top 20 Lists
✓ New Green Heroes & Corporate Villains
✓ Best (★) & Worst (☠) picks in the charts

Let's reclaim our democracy.

THE WEBSITE

This guide is far too small to contain the wide range of data used to generate rankings for each company. If you are interested in more specifics on how individual companies are rated, and exactly what is taken into account, you can visit the website. It also contains updated ratings, direct links to resources, and new product categories that have been added since the writing of this guide.

I will also note that there is now a smartphone app available on iOS and Android phones. "Better World Shopper" based on the same data as this book. While it does not provide all of the useful information you'll find in this guide, it does give you instant access to all of the rankings. Having this information at your fingertips can turn out to be really useful, particularly when you forget to bring the book with you!

Learn more about the research behind this work and take a peek at the app online at

www.betterworldshopper.org

THE PROBLEM

Money is power. Perhaps more than any generation that has come before us, we understand the deeply rooted reality of this short phrase and its universal meaning for every human being living on this planet.

It follows that wherever large amounts of money collect, so also new centers of power form. The latest historical manifestation of this is the modern corporation. As trillions of dollars accumulate in the corporate sphere, we witness the growing power of corporations to shape the world as they see fit.

This power is not limited to controlling the face of our own government through consistent, record-breaking campaign contributions, but also the fate of millions of people and the planet itself through jobs, resource exploitation, pollution, working conditions, energy consumption, forest destruction, and so on.

Make no mistake, these new power centers are not democracies. We don't vote for the CEOs or their policies (unless we are rich enough to be significant shareholders who are informed enough to know what's going on and compassionate enough to care about more than just personal profit), yet our destinies are increasingly in their hands.

THE SOLUTION

As these power centers shift, we must shift our own voices if we wish to be heard. As citizens, on average, we might vote once every four years, if at all. As consumers, we vote every single day with the purest form of power...money. The average American family spends around $22,000 every year on goods and services. Think of it as casting 22,000 votes every year for the kind of world you want to live in.

Unfortunately, as difficult as it is to find good, solid information on candidates during an election year, it's often even harder to find good, solid information on corporations. Our current laws are so lax that half of the time we can't even figure out which brands belong to which companies (they don't have to tell us), much less have any idea of what their business practices look like.

For the past decade, I've dedicated myself to researching this very problem by compiling a database of every reliable source of information available on corporate behavior and synthesizing the information into a single report card grade for every company. The result is this book. Use it to reclaim your true vote. Use it to build a better world.

THE ISSUES

➢ **HUMAN RIGHTS:** child labor, sweatshops, slavery, worker health and safety records, human trafficking, developing-world exploitation, international health issues, economic divestment, union busting, fair trade, worker fatalities, livable wages, democratic principles.

➢ **THE ENVIRONMENT:** climate change, renewable energy, toxic waste dumping, recycling, eco-innovations, sustainable farming, ocean conservation, rainforest destruction, ecosystem impacts, overall pollution.

➢ **ANIMAL PROTECTION:** humane treatment, factory farming, animal habitat preservation, sustainable seafood harvesting, animal testing, animal-free alternatives, vegan-friendliness.

➢ **COMMUNITY INVOLVEMENT:** family farms, nonprofit alliances, local businesses, sustainable growth, campaign contributions, paid lobbyists, political corruption, greenwashing, transparency.

➢ **SOCIAL JUSTICE:** harassment, discrimination (based on race, gender, age, sexuality, ability, religion, ethnicity), class-action lawsuits, unethical business practices, government fines, cover-ups, illegal activities, executive pay.

THE SOURCES

Here is a list of a few of the resources used to assess the overall social and environmental responsibility of the companies in this guide:

[AH] American Humane Association
[ASB] American Sustainable Business Council
[AYS] As You Sow: CEO Salaries & Packaging
[CCC] Clean Clothes Campaign
[CC] Climate Counts: Global Warming Score
[CER] CERES: Climate Change Research
[CRP] Center for Responsive Politics
[CSP] Center for Science in the Public Interest
[CW] Corpwatch: Greenwash Awards
[EC] Ethical Consumer: Rankings & Boycotts
[EPA] US Environmental Protection Agency
[FTF] Fair Trade Federation: FT Certified
[FTW] Free2Work: Human Trafficking
[GAM] Green America: Certified Green Business
[GP] Greenpeace: Sustainable Seafood
[HRC] Human Rights Campaign: Equality Index
[ILRF] International Labor Rights Forum
[OXF] Oxfam International
[PERI] Political Economy Research Institute
[RS] Responsible Shopper: Ethical Rankings
[SAI] Social Accountability International
[SEC] Securites and Exchange Commission
[SVN] Social Venture Network
[SVT] Silicon Valley Toxics Coalition
[UCS] Union of Concerned Scientists

For a more comprehensive list visit: www.betterworldshopper.org.

THE RANKINGS

STEP 1: Over 25 years' worth of data has been collected from a wide range of public, private, and nonprofit sources, tracking information on one or more of the five issue areas that make up the overall responsibility picture for companies that create the products and services we use every day.

STEP 2: The data is organized into a massive database of more than 2,000 companies that matches each individual company with its brands; assigns appropriate weights to each piece of data based on its quality, reliability, and scope; and calculates an overall social and environmental responsibility score for each company from –100 to +100.

STEP 3: Companies and brands are transferred to smaller, more specific data charts based on common product categories, where each is assigned a letter grade based on its overall responsibility. This highly organized grading system allows consumers to maximize the impact of their dollars regardless of what they're purchasing.

THE RANKINGS

STEP 4: Researchers are sent to supermarkets, natural foods stores, and retail outlets across the country to identify those products that are most commonly available to the average consumer to make sure that what you see on the shelves matches what you see in the book. Those particular companies and brands are then transferred into the easy-to-use report cards that make up the bulk of the shopping guide.

STEP 5: As regular data sources release their latest findings, they are added to the database. Also, as new third-party sources of data are identified, they are evaluated for potential inclusion in the ranking system. Mergers and buyouts are tracked so that their effects on the rankings can be noted. Updated rankings are regularly made available online through the website until a new edition of the shopping guide can be published.

As readers, your comments and suggestions are invaluable. Please contact me if you have ideas on how to improve the ranking system.

contact@betterworldshopper.org

FREQUENTLY ASKED QUESTIONS

"Isn't it more important to buy less stuff rather than worry about the kind of stuff we're buying?": Both are equally important. As we've learned from the voluntary simplicity movement, we must reduce our *quantity* of consumption if we are to have any reasonable future. At the same time, we must increase the *quality* of our consumption so that every dollar spent helps build a better tomorrow rather than bring about its destruction. While I wholeheartedly support the former, this book deals mainly with the latter.

"What if I don't have access to or can't afford many of the products that receive 'A' ratings?": Don't give up! It's important to choose the best option available to you depending on your location and resources, both of which will likely change many times in your life. Sometimes the choice is between a 'C' brand and an 'F' brand, and that is just as important a choice to make. I, myself, strive to maintain an overall shopping GPA of 'B+' - and even then, I'm not always successful. Remember, as with voting, there is always a choice to be made, imperfect as it may be.

FREQUENTLY ASKED QUESTIONS

"Isn't this 'buying green' just something to make us feel better rather than something that will actually lead to real change?": No. Trillions of dollars circulate in the global economy, driven primarily by consumers. These are our dollars that are shaping the fate of this world, and we must begin taking responsibility for their collective impact. Dollars (like votes) add up very quickly and can lead to powerful changes in both the short and long term.

"Shouldn't we be voting, demonstrating, and organizing within our political system?": Yes. We need to bring transparency, accountability, and responsibility to both our political AND economic systems. If we address only one, our efforts will ultimately fail. So, do not use this guide as an excuse to shift focus away from our political problems — the two go hand in hand.

"How do I find out more details about a particular company or the ranking system as a whole?": Email me, or better yet, invite me out to come talk about it!

BEST COMPANY PROFILE (BANKS)

NEW RESOURCE BANK

- ☆ Green America Certified Green Business
- ☆ San Francisco Certified Green Business
- ☆ Social Venture Network member
- ☆ A Certified "B Corporation"
- ☆ 100% Wind Power, EPA Certified
- ☆ LEED Gold Certified headquarters
- ☆ American Sustainable Business Council member
- ☆ Car-sharing program offered to all employees for meetings
- ☆ Offers a debit card that donates to environmental orgs with each purchase

OVERALL GRADE: A+

www.newresourcebank.com

WORST COMPANY PROFILE (BANKS)

CITIBANK

- Recipient, Corporate Shame Award[6]
- Worst overall ranking in industry[61]
- Worst Corporations List for two years[51]
- 'D' for social & environmental impacts[61]
- Overall ethics rating of VERY POOR[30]
- $50 billion paid by taxpayers to bailout[54]
- $113 million paid to political lobbyists[12]
- $39 million in campaign contributions[12]
- $2.7 billion to settle WorldCom fraud[54]
- SEC — Citi helped Enron commit fraud[48]
- Sued for selling worthless Enron stock[61]
- Paid largest settlement in FTC history[48]
- GAO — negligent of money laundering[73]
- $70 million paid for unfair lending[61]

OVERALL GRADE: F

For more details you can look up the source reference number in the DATA SOURCES section in the back of this book.

THE 20 BEST LIST

1. NEW BELGIUM BREWING
2. SEVENTH GENERATION
3. ORGANIC VALLEY
4. PATAGONIA
5. ALTER ECO
6. DR. BRONNER'S
7. METHOD
8. EQUAL EXCHANGE
9. TRADITIONAL MEDICINALS
10. ECOVER
11. KLEAN KANTEEN
12. CLIF BAR
13. EO PRODUCTS
14. NATURE'S PATH
15. G DIAPERS
16. NANCY'S ORGANIC CREAMERY
17. MAGGIE'S ORGANICS
18. EDEN FOODS
19. DANSKO
20. KING ARTHUR FLOUR

Rankings are based on overall social and environmental records

THE 20 WORST LIST

1. EXXON-MOBIL
2. KRAFT HEINZ
3. WALMART
4. CHEVRON-TEXACO
5. GENERAL MOTORS
6. GENERAL ELECTRIC
7. PFIZER
8. NESTLÉ
9. CITIBANK
10. DOW CHEMICAL
11. VERIZON
12. BLUE CROSS / BLUE SHIELD
13. MICROSOFT
14. AT&T
15. COCA COLA
16. FORD
17. MONSANTO
18. COMCAST
19. KOCH INDUSTRIES
20. ABBOTT LABORATORIES

Rankings are based on overall social and environmental records

THE 10 SMALL BUT BEAUTIFUL LIST

1. GUAYAKI
2. BETTER WORLD TELECOM
3. NEW RESOURCE BANK
4. NEW LEAF PAPER
5. NUMI TEA
6. BETTER WORLD CLUB
7. PRESERVE (RECYCLINE)
8. GROUNDS FOR CHANGE
9. NUTIVA
10. TS DESIGNS

The above list includes 10 small companies you may not have heard of that are true social and environmental leaders in their industries.

THE TOP 10 THINGS TO CHANGE

1. BANK
2. GASOLINE
3. SUPERMARKET
4. RETAIL STORES
5. CAR
6. SEAFOOD
7. CHOCOLATE
8. COFFEE / TEA
9. CREDIT CARDS
10. CLEANING PRODUCTS

If you want to begin with the changes that will make the most difference for people and the planet, start with these ten things.

THE 10 BIGGEST SUCCESS STORIES

GRADE CHANGE	*'06 ▸ '17*
1. EO PRODUCTS	B+ ▸ A+
2. GREEN FOREST	B ▸ A+
3. SAN-J	C ▸ A
4. GAP CLOTHING	C+ ▸ B+
5. SOUTHWEST AIR	D+ ▸ B+
6. DANSKO	** ▸ A+
7. METHOD	** ▸ A+
8. PANGEA ORGANICS	** ▸ A+
9. KIMPTON HOTELS	** ▸ A+
10. CHIPOTLE	** ▸ A

The above list includes the five companies that, as of June 2017, have shown the most improvement since the first edition of the book was released, as well as five companies that weren't listed in the original edition (noted by **). Every one of these companies is a demonstration of what a deep commitment to a better world can achieve in a mere eight years.

THE 10 BIGGEST DISAPPOINTMENTS

GRADE CHANGE	*'06 ▸ '17*
1. SILK	A+ ▸ B-
2. HORIZON ORGANIC	A ▸ C
3. BURT'S BEES	A- ▸ C+
4. BP	A- ▸ D-
5. FEDEX	B ▸ D
6. CADBURY	B- ▸ F
7. GERBER	C+ ▸ F
8. UNILEVER	C ▸ D
9. PROCTER & GAMBLE	C ▸ F
10. BANK OF AMERICA	C- ▸ F

The above list includes the 10 companies that, as of June 2017, have fallen from the top of their respective industries to the middle, or worse, from the middle to the very bottom. It is essential that we, as consumers, send a clear message that we will no longer reward companies for this kind of irresponsible behavior.

THE TOP 10 BAILOUT LIST

1.	AIG	70
2.	CITIBANK	50
3.	BANK OF AMERICA	45
4.	GENERAL MOTORS	31
5.	JP MORGAN	25
6.	WELLS FARGO	25
7.	CHRYSLER	12
8.	MORGAN STANLEY	10
9.	GOLDMAN SACHS	10
10.	PNC FINANCIAL	8

We are quickly learning that unless we, as consumers, can keep companies responsible in the marketplace, we may end up paying for their irresponsible behavior with our own taxpayer dollars.

The above list includes the 10 companies that (by mid-2009) had received the most bailout money from the US taxpayers. The figures on the right represent how much we have spent, *in billions*, bailing these companies out.[54]

THE TOP 10 LOBBYIST LIST

1.	GENERAL ELECTRIC	348
2.	AT&T	339
3.	KRAFT HEINZ	329
4.	BLUE CROSS/SHIELD	303
5.	EXXON MOBIL	247
6.	VERIZON	245
7.	GENERAL MOTORS	174
8.	PFIZER	171
9.	COMCAST	171
10.	MICROSOFT	150

It's important to understand that we are not the only ones learning to turn our dollars into votes. These are some of the loudest economic voices in Washington.

The above list includes 10 companies currently spending some of the largest amounts of money on Washington lobbyists to influence the democratic process in ways that serve their own interests. The figures on the right represent how much they have spent, *in millions*, over the past fifteen years.[12]

WHO OWNS WHO?

COMPANY	*OWNED BY*
1. WHOLE FOODS	AMAZON
2. SEVENTH GEN	UNILEVER
3. BURT'S BEES	CLOROX
4. TOM'S OF MAINE	COLGATE
5. STONYFIELD	DANONE
6. BEN & JERRY'S	UNILEVER
7. AVEDA	L'OREAL
8. NEW CHAPTER	P & G
9. HONEST TEA	COCA COLA
10. ANNIE'S	GEN MILLS

The above list includes the 10 companies that people are most surprised to find out are owned by larger companies that don't always share the values of the former.

Don't assume, however, that these companies are no longer socially and environmentally responible. According to the data, many of them have maintained most or all of their social and environmental responsibility.

INDEPENDENTLY OWNED

1. CLIF
2. DR. BRONNER'S
3. NEW BELGIUM BREWING
4. EQUAL EXCHANGE
5. ORGANIC VALLEY
6. PATAGONIA
7. KLEAN KANTEEN
8. NATURE'S PATH
9. EDEN FOODS
10. CHIPOTLE

The above list includes 10 companies that have yet to be purchased by larger multinational corporations with unknown intentions. While our financial system currently incentivizes purchasing smaller companies as an effective "growth strategy," the results are not always best for consumers or citizens.

These 10 companies could "cash out" at any point, but for now, they are holding on to their independence despite the odds.

WHAT DO THE GRADES MEAN?

A	Often these companies were created specifically to provide socially and environmentally responsible options for consumers. Others are responsibility leaders in their area. [★ = your best choice.]
B	These tend to represent mainstream companies that are making significant progress in turning toward more people/planet-friendly behaviors.
C	Companies that fall in the middle either have mixed responsibility records or insufficient data exists to rank them relative to the other companies. The latter are listed in italics to differentiate them from the former.
D	If a company ends up here, it is involved in practices that have significantly negative consequences for humans and the environment.
F	This category is reserved for companies that are actively participating in the rapid destruction of the planet and the exploitation of human beings. Avoid these products at all costs. [☠ = your worst choice.]

WHAT IS ALL THIS EXTRA STUFF?

WHAT YOU NEED TO KNOW

This section will give you a thumbnail sketch of the current industry and its impact.

BUYING TIPS

Here you'll see tips that should help you maximize the positive impact of your dollar.

GREEN HERO

Company X

Examples (☆) of just a few of the things that put this particular company head and shoulders above the rest.

CORPORATE VILLAIN

Company Y

Examples (☠) of some of the things that land this company squarely at the bottom of the rankings (cited in the Data Sources section).

USEFUL RESOURCES

Here you'll find web links to sites that provide you with reliable data about the companies in the industry you're examining.

WHAT IF I CAN'T FIND A COMPANY?

While this guide is meant to be comprehensive, it is far from complete. You will likely encounter companies and brands on the shelves that don't show up in these pages. Here are a few simple guidelines that should help you:

If an unknown company's products are certified *fair trade*, you may assume that it falls into the A- range.

If an unknown company's products are certified *organic*, you may assume that it falls into the B+ range.

If you don't know anything at all about a particular company or brand, assume that it falls into the C range.

Unknown companies producing clothing, electronics, or shoes should be assumed to have a D or F.

If you wish to see a more detailed version of these rankings or ask about a particular company that you can't find in the guide, you're welcome to visit

www.betterworldshopper.org.

HOW TO USE THIS SHOPPING GUIDE

This book is meant to be used as a practical guide while shopping at the supermarket, in the mall, or online. Familiarize yourself with the alphabetical listing of categories and "dog-ear" any pages you find particularly useful.

Utilize the rankings on the left as a quick guide to any product you're thinking about buying. Note that all rankings are relative to their product category, so a company may shift up or down depending on its competition.

Useful information and helpful tips appear on the right along with a quick sketch of some of the differences between the best and worst companies. At the bottom of the page are links to online resources to learn more about some of the companies listed.

The book has been purposefully made small so that you can keep it with you in your purse, backpack, briefcase, or pocket. Find a convenient place for it now, while you're reading this sentence. Whatever you do, don't put it on a shelf!

AIRLINES

A	A+	
	A	
	A–	
B	B+	★JetBlue, Southwest
	B	Alaska Air, Horizon
	B–	Frontier, Virgin
C	C+	KLM, Air France, Spirit, Easy Jet
	C	Cathay Pacific, Qantas, Singapore, Japan Airlines, Lufthansa, British Airways
	C–	Korean Air, SAS, AirTran, Aer Lingus, Air Canada, Air New Zealand, Express Jet, Sky West
D	D+	
	D	Delta
	D–	
F	F	☠ United, Continental, US Airways, American Airlines, American Eagle

AIRLINES

WHAT YOU NEED TO KNOW

Air travel has become so ubiquitous in our modern society that we often forget its significant environmental impact.

BUYING TIPS

✓ Many online travel organizations now offer carbon offsets to offset your flight's greenhouse gas emissions. (See TRAVEL.)

GREEN HERO

JetBlue

☆ Perfect 100 on HRC Equality Index
☆ Industry leader in treatment of passengers
☆ Offers carbon offsets & green food options

CORPORATE VILLAIN

United

☠ RS "F" for recycling efforts in the industry[61]
☠ Paid $73 million to Washington lobbyists[12]
☠ Named global climate change laggard[15]

USEFUL RESOURCES

💻 sustainabletravelinternational.org

APPLIANCES & HARDWARE

A	A+	★Preserve, Recycline, TerraCycle
	A	Old Fashioned Milk Paint
	A–	
B	B+	Ace Hardware
	B	WD-40,
	B–	Electrolux, Frigidaire, Norelco, Cuisinart, Conair
C	C+	Dyson
	C	Miele, Tefal, DeWalt, JCB, Wahl, BSH, Dremel, RYOBI, DeLonghi, Siemens, Sunbeam, Haier, Black & Decker, Stanley, Sony, Krups, *Bissell, Dirt Devil, Tupperware, Hoover, Magic Chef*
	C–	Kitchenaid, Admiral, Maytag, Owens Corning, Sylvania, Whirlpool, LG, Sherwin Williams, Acme, Dutch Boy, Sanyo, Bosch
D	D+	3M
	D	Daewoo, Philips, Braun, Panasonic, Hitachi, Samsung
	D–	Home Depot, Lowe's, Emerson
F	F	☠ Walmart, Sears, Kenmore, ☠ GE, Craftsman, Costco

APPLIANCES & HARDWARE

WHAT YOU NEED TO KNOW

Whether it's major home improvement efforts or just small kitchen appliances, the hardware you buy for your house has a significant impact on the people abroad who help manufacture it.

BUYING TIPS

✓ Look for products with Energy Star labels

CORPORATE VILLAIN

Walmart

- ☠ MM's "Worst Corporation" list for three years[51]
- ☠ Major toxic waste dumping fines[25]
- ☠ CEP "F" for overall social responsibility[14]
- ☠ Documented exploitation of child labor[61]

CORPORATE VILLAIN

GE (General Electric)

- ☠ MM's "Worst Corporation" list for five years[51]
- ☠ #34 in "Top 100 Corporate Criminals"[51]
- ☠ Target of "War Profiteer" campaign[61]
- ☠ Paid $348 million to Washington lobbyists[12]

USEFUL RESOURCES

💻 www.energystar.gov

BABY CARE

A	A+	★Seventh Generation, ★gDiapers, Plum Organics
	A	Earth Mama, Peapods, Happy Baby, Healthy Times, Ella's Kitchen
	A−	Organic Baby, Tender Care, Tushies
B	B+	Weleda, Earth's Best, Jäsön
	B	Huggies, GoodNites, Baby Magic
	B−	Mr. Bubble,
C	C+	Playtex, Nature's Gate
	C	Graco, Horizon Organic, BeechNut, Bourdreaux's, Burt's Bees, *Munchkin*
	C−	Avent, Oshkosh, Britax, Chicco, Evenflo, Playmates, Carter's, Nature's Goodness
D	D+	Babies R Us
	D	Church & Dwight, Arm & Hammer, Del Monte, Enfamil, QTips, Vaseline
	D−	Coppertone, Chiquita, Johnson & Johnson, Aveeno, Baby Einstein, Disney
F	F	☠ Gerber, Nestlé, Nabisco, Pampers, Pedialyte, Pediasure, Similac, Luvs

BABY CARE

WHAT YOU NEED TO KNOW

Infants and toddlers are more vulnerable to the effects of harmful chemicals and pesticides, so if you're going to buy anything organic, it should be something from this category.

GREEN HERO

Seventh Generation

☆ Ranked #2 best company on the planet
☆ Empowers consumers w/packaging
☆ Winner, Sustainability Report Award
☆ Socially Responsible Business Award

GREEN HERO

gDiapers

☆ B Lab Certified Responsible Company
☆ GAM certified Green Business
☆ Developed cloth/disposable hybrid diaper

CORPORATE VILLAIN

Gerber (Nestlé)

☠ Baby formula human rights boycott[48]
☠ "Most Irresponsible" corporation award[6]
☠ Involved in child slavery lawsuit[61]
☠ Aggressive takeovers of family farms[61]

BAKED GOODS & BAKING SUPPLIES

A	A+	★King Arthur, Eden, ★Nature's Path
	A	Bob's Red Mill,
	A–	Spectrum, Ener-G, Rapunzel, Hain, Arrowhead Mills
B	B+	Vermont Bread, Hodgson Mill
	B	Betty Crocker, Pillsbury, Progresso, Quaker, Gold Medal, Bisquick
	B–	Sun-Maid
C	C+	Ghirardelli, Krusteaz
	C	Mother's, Dr. Oetker, *Karo, Entenmann's*
	C–	Eagle Brand, Little Debbie
D	D+	Hostess
	D	Keebler, Kellogg's, Arm & Hammer, Contadina, Cake Mate, Diamond
	D–	Hershey's, Banquet, Borden
F	F	☠ Jell-O, Kraft, Planters, Nestlé, Carnation, Duncan Hines, Nabisco, Albers, Libby's

BAKED GOODS & BAKING SUPPLIES

BUYING TIPS

✓ Buy organic baking products when available

GREEN HERO

King Arthur Flour

☆ 100% employee-owned company
☆ Awarded "Most Democratic Workplace"
☆ Business Ethics award winner
☆ B Lab Certified Responsible Company
☆ BBB's Torch Award for ethics

GREEN HERO

Nature's Path

☆ GAM certified Green Business
☆ Named one of Canada's Greenest Employers
☆ Sponsors environmental efforts and festivals

CORPORATE VILLAIN

Jell-O (Kraft)

☠ MM's "Worst Corporation" list for five years[51]
☠ Currently target of two major boycotts[22,55]
☠ Greenwash Award for public deception[25]
☠ Named global climate change laggard[15]
☠ Paid $329 million to Washington lobbyists[12]

BANKS & CREDIT CARDS

A	A+	★New Resource Bank, One Pacific Coast, Sunrise Banks, Vancity
	A	Alternatives FCU, Green Choice, City First, Albina, First Green Bank
	A–	Working Assets CC, Green America CC, Brighter Planet CC
B	B+	
	B	LOCAL CREDIT UNIONS
	B–	American Express, TD Bank, ING, Northern Trust
C	C+	Deutsche Bank
	C	MasterCard, Sovereign, Santander, Capital One
	C–	KeyBank, Comerica, Discover
D	D+	Fifth Third, Citizens
	D	SunTrust, VISA, Credit Suisse, Royal Bank of Scotland, US Bank, HSBC
	D–	Chase, JP Morgan, UBS, Barclay's
F	F	☠ Citibank, Bank of America, Wells Fargo, Goldman Sachs

BANKS & CREDIT CARDS

WHAT YOU NEED TO KNOW

Where you put your money when you're not spending it is just as important as responsibly choosing what you spend it on. For your whole life (even while you sleep), that money will either be building a better world or tearing it down. Small, local banks and credit unions are typically your best bet. While shopping, make each purchase doubly effective by using a credit card (CC) that donates a percentage of your purchases (over $5,500/yr for the average American) to saving the planet.

BUYING TIPS

✓ Try using both a local bank AND an 'A' bank
✓ Find out which credit unions are in your area
✓ Switch to a socially responsible credit card

GREEN HERO & CORPORATE VILLAIN

✓ Detailed profiles on pages 12–13

USEFUL RESOURCES

💻 www.creditunion.coop/cu_locator
💻 www.breakupwithyourmegabank.org

BEER

A	**A+**	★New Belgium
	A	★Sierra Nevada, Brewery Vivant, Hopworks, Bison, Otter Creek
	A–	LOCAL MICROBREWERIES, Odell, Alaskan, Brooklyn, Great Lakes
B	**B+**	Allagash, Eel River, Stone, Anderson Valley, Boulevard, Bell's, Uinta
	B	Long Trail, Harpoon, Anchor Steam, Kona, Widmer, Full Sail
	B–	Samuel Smith's
C	**C+**	Pabst, Stroh's, Schlitz
	C	Newcastle, Heineken, Amstel, Asahi
	C–	
D	**D+**	Samuel Adams
	D	Keystone, Molson, Carlsberg, Blue Moon, Leinenkugel, Guinness, Old Milwaukee, Coors, Foster's, Miller
	D–	☠ Budweiser, Michelob, Rolling Rock, Becks, Stella Artois, Bass, Busch, Lowenbrau, Harp, Natural Light, Modelo, Pacifico, Corona
F	**F**	

BEER

BUYING TIPS

✓ Look for organic varieties of beer
✓ Buy from local microbreweries when possible
✓ Avoid buying beer in plastic bottles

GREEN HERO

New Belgium

☆ 1st 100% wind-powered brewery
☆ Conserves 50% more water vs. average
☆ An employee-owned business
☆ 4x awarded "Most Democratic Workplace"
☆ $1.6 million donated to local community

GREEN HERO

Sierra Nevada

☆ Designated Climate Action Leader
☆ Numerous environmental awards
☆ Recycles 98% of waste created in production

CORPORATE VILLAIN

Budweiser (Anheuser-Busch InBev)

☠ Paid $55 million to Washington lobbyists[12]
☠ EC overall responsibility rating of POOR[30]
☠ US govt sued over monopolistic practices[54]

BODY CARE

A	A+	★Pangea Organics, Preserve, Dr. Bronner's, Method, Tweezerman, Aubrey Organics, Eco Lips, EO
	A	Aveda, Auromere, Aura Cacia, Zia, Nubius, Kiss My Face, Badger
	A–	Tom's of Maine, Allen's Naturally, Dr. Hauschka, Weleda, Jäsön, Alba
B	B+	Lush, BWC
	B	Shikai, Body Shop, Colgate, Speed Stick, Mennen, Ecco Bella, Crystal
	B–	CO Bigelow, Carmex, Shikai
C	C+	Bic, Burt's Bees, Nature's Gate
	C	Jergens, Biore, Ban, Banana Boat, Avalon Organics, Hawaiian Tropic, Schick, Edge, *Sure, Barbasol, Blistex*
	C–	Nivea
D	D+	Curel
	D	Coppertone, Keri, Dove, Suave, Vaseline, Degree, Axe, Q-Tips
	D–	Arrid, Arm & Hammer, Neutrogena, Lubriderm, Aveeno, Clean & Clear, Purell, Right Guard, Dry Idea
F	F	☠ Chapstick, Mitchum, Oil of Olay, ☠ Secret, Gillette, Noxema, Old Spice

BODY CARE

BUYING TIPS

✓ Avoid products tested on animals
✓ Seek out items made with organic ingredients
✓ Look for recyclable containers — #1, #2 plastic
✓ Buy larger quantities to reduce packaging

GREEN HERO

Pangea Organics

☆ GAM certified Green Business
☆ Never tests ingredients on animals
☆ 2x award winner for Business Ethics

CORPORATE VILLAIN

Chapstick (Pfizer)

☠ #64 of PERI 100 Most Toxic Water Polluters[58]
☠ #17 in "Top 100 Corporate Criminals"[51]
☠ MM's "Worst Corporation" list for four years[51]
☠ Paid $171 million to Washington lobbyists[12]

CORPORATE VILLAIN

Secret (Procter & Gamble)

☠ MM's "Worst Corporation" list for two years[51]
☠ Continues unnecessary animal testing[10]
☠ "Bottom Rung," Ladder of Responsibility[40]
☠ Spent over $68 million on lobbyists[12]

BREAD

A	**A+**	LOCAL BAKERY
	A	★Alvarado St Bakery
	A–	Ener-G, Rudi's Organic, Vermont Bread Co., Great Harvest Bread Co.
B	**B+**	Food For Life
	B	Betty Crocker, Gold Medal, Colombo, Pillsbury
	B–	Sun-Maid
C	**C+**	La Brea
	C	Pepperidge Farm, *Country Hearth, Lender's, Van De Kamp's, Milton's, FiberOne, Roman Meal, Mission, Wonder, Home Pride, Nature's Pride*
	C–	Weight Watchers
D	**D+**	
	D	
	D–	Alexia, Boboli, Oroweat, Tia Rosa, Thomas', Arnold, Freihofer's
F	**F**	☠ Rainbo, Kraft, Stove-Top, Earth Grains, Sara Lee

BREAD

WHAT YOU NEED TO KNOW

Despite all of our technological advancement, it's still a challenge to find a good, socially responsible loaf of bread in the supermarket.

BUYING TIPS

✓ Support a local bakery in your community

GREEN HERO

Alvarado Street Bakery

☆ Worker-owned cooperative
☆ PC Socially Responsible Business Award
☆ GAM certified Green Business

CORPORATE VILLAIN

Rainbo (Tyson)

☠ CEP "F" for overall social responsibility[14]
☠ Paid $23 million to Washington lobbyists[12]
☠ MM's "Worst Corporation" list for two years[51]
☠ Violation of Foreign Corrupt Practices Act[71]

USEFUL RESOURCES

💻 www.cornucopia.org/cereal-scorecard
💻 www.responsibleshopper.org

BREAKFAST FOOD

A	A+	
	A	★Tofurky, ★Amy's Kitchen
	A–	
B	B+	Ian's
	B	Udi's, General Mills, Betty Crocker, Pillsbury
	B–	
C	C+	Krusteaz
	C	Quaker, Aunt Jemima, *Entenmann's, Armour, Log Cabin, Mrs. Butterworth's, Bird's Eye, Swanson*
	C–	Smucker's, Hungry Jack, Bob Evans, Weight Watchers
D	D+	
	D	Kellogg's, Morningstar Farms, Eggo, Kashi, Hormel, Ore-Ida, Skippy, Golden Griddle
	D–	PAM, Banquet
F	F	☠Jimmy Dean, Tyson, Nestlé, Kraft, Nabisco, Boca

BREAKFAST FOOD

WHAT YOU NEED TO KNOW

Every morning of your life, what you put on your plate for breakfast will determine what kind of world your children inherit in the future.

BUYING TIPS

✓ Buy at least one organic item for breakfast

GREEN HERO

Tofurky (Turtle Island)

☆ EPA Certified 100% Green Power
☆ Highest standards of organic integrity
☆ 1st food sponsor of The Humane Society

GREEN HERO

Amy's Kitchen

☆ Donates food to relief efforts
☆ Produces all-vegetarian, organic foods
☆ GAM certified Green Business

CORPORATE VILLAIN

Jimmy Dean (Tyson)

☠ #52 in "Top 100 Corporate Criminals"[51]
☠ Violation of Foreign Corrupt Practices Act[71]
☠ CEP "F" for overall social responsibility[14]
☠ Paid $23 million to Washington lobbyists[12]

BUTTER & MARGARINE

A	A+	★Organic Valley, Organic Pastures, Straus Family Creamery
	A	
	A–	Cabot, Spectrum
B	B+	
	B	Clover Stornetta, Smart Balance, Earth Balance
	B–	
C	C+	
	C	Horizon Organic, Kerrygold, *Nucoa, Challenge, Canoleo, Saffola, Canola Harvest, Cloverleaf*
	C–	
D	D+	
	D	Land O' Lakes, Brummel & Brown, I Can't Believe It's Not Butter, Shedd's, Country Crock, Promise, Imperial
	D–	☠ Parkay, ConAgra, Blue Bonnet, Fleischmann's, Benecol
F	F	

BUTTER & MARGARINE

BUYING TIPS

✓ Look for "No Hormones" and "No Antibiotics"
✓ Seek out items made with organic ingredients
✓ Avoid hydrogenated, saturated, and trans fats

GREEN HERO

Organic Valley

☆ Small family farmer-owned co-operative
☆ Gives 10% of profits to local community
☆ Humane animal treatment a priority
☆ Ranked #3 best company on the planet

CORPORATE VILLAIN

Parkay (ConAgra)

☠ #50 in "Top 100 Corporate Criminals"[51]
☠ CEP "F" for overall social responsibility[14]
☠ Ceres "Climate Change Laggard"[15]
☠ Lobbied against GMO Labeling[21]

USEFUL RESOURCES

💻 www.organicconsumers.org
💻 www.cornucopia.org/dairy_brand_ratings
💻 www.localharvest.org

CANDY, GUM & MINTS

A	A+	
	A	★Glee Gum, Sencha Natural
	A–	Hain, Speakeasy, St. Claire's
B	B+	Ginger People
	B	Newman's Own
	B–	Red Vines
C	C+	Panda, Haribo, La Vie
	C	Tootsie Roll, *Charm's, Mike & Ike, Werthers, Tic Tacs, Mentos, Andes*
	C–	Jelly Belly
D	D+	
	D	
	D–	Hershey's, Heath, Mounds, Reese's, Kit Kat, Almond Joy, Twizzlers
F	F	☠ M&Ms, Twix, Starburst, Skittles, Snickers, Milky Way, 3 Musketeers, LifeSavers, Mars, Extra, Orbit, Big Red, Kraft, Cadbury, Nerds, Nestlé, Butterfinger, Wonka, SweeTarts, After Eight, Certs, Dentyne, Trident, Wrigley's

CANDY, GUM & MINTS

BUYING TIPS

Most major candy manufacturers are also major chocolate purchasers, which currently means that they are using child slave labor to produce much of their candy. It's important to keep these companies accountable until they agree to basic human rights standards in the industry.

GREEN HERO

Glee Gum

☆ GAM certified Green Business
☆ Uses wild-harvested rainforest plants
☆ Actively supports environmental groups

CORPORATE VILLAIN

M&Ms (Mars)

☠ On MM's "10 Worst Corporations" list[51]
☠ Evidence of involvement in child slave labor[61]
☠ Target of international fair trade campaign[25]
☠ Paid $36 million to Washington lobbyists[12]

USEFUL RESOURCES

- www.greenpages.org
- www.globalexchange.org

CANNED GOODS

A	A+	★Eden Foods
	A	Amy's Kitchen
	A–	Walnut Acres, Westbrae, Bearitos, Native Forest
B	B+	
	B	Muir Glen, Old El Paso, Hamburger Helper, Progresso, Green Giant,
	B–	Sunsweet, Tree Top, Santa Cruz Organic
C	C+	
	C	Campbell's, *Bush's, B&M, Nalley, Ortega, GOYA*
	C–	Ocean Spray
D	D+	Mott's
	D	Del Monte, S&W, Contadina, Hormel, Dinty Moore, La Victoria, Stagg, Heinz, Knorr, Dole, French's
	D–	Dennison's, Rosarita, Van Camp's, Marie Callender's, Hunt's
F	F	☠ Libby's, Taco Bell

CANNED GOODS

WHAT YOU NEED TO KNOW

Some of the most socially responsible companies now provide a wide variety of canned goods that should be available at most supermarkets.

GREEN HERO

Eden Foods

- ☆ Ranked #18 best company on the planet
- ☆ CEP's highest social responsibility score
- ☆ GAM certified Green Business

CORPORATE VILLAIN

Libby's (Kraft)

- ☠ Greenwash Award for public deception[25]
- ☠ Named global climate change laggard[15]
- ☠ Currently target of two major boycotts[22,55]
- ☠ Paid $329 million to Washington lobbyists[12]
- ☠ MM's "Worst Corporation" list for five years[51]

USEFUL RESOURCES

- 💻 www.responsibleshopper.org
- 💻 www.ethicalconsumer.org

CARS

A	A+	
	A	
	A–	
B	B+	★Honda, Acura
	B	Toyota, Lexus, Scion, Hyundai, Kia
	B–	
C	C+	Subaru,
	C	Smart Car, Peugeot, Renault, *Tesla*
	C–	Nissan, Infiniti, Mazda, Mini, Volvo, Fiat, Porsche, BMW, Tata, Ferrari, Mercedes, Suzuki, Saab
D	D+	
	D	Volkswagen, Audi, Isuzu
	D–	Mitsubishi
F	F	☠ General Motors, Ford, Jeep, GMC, ☠ Chrysler, Lincoln, Buick, Cadillac, Saturn, Chevrolet, Dodge, Hummer, Jaguar, Land Rover, Mercury

CARS

BUYING TIPS:

✓ Look for cars that get at least 30 mpg
✓ Think about a hybrid vehicle for your next car
✓ Consider buying carbon offsets for your car

GREEN HERO

Honda

☆ UCS excellent environmental auto ranking
☆ CERES named as climate sustainability leader
☆ Top eco-ranking from Greenopia

CORPORATE VILLAIN

General Motors

☠ Leader in fighting clean air legislation[61]
☠ Paid $174 million to Washington lobbyists[12]
☠ MM's "Worst Corporation" list for four years[51]
☠ *$31 billion* paid by taxpayers to bailout[54]

CORPORATE VILLAIN

Chrysler

☠ UCS worst environmental auto ranking[69]
☠ Paid $47 million to Washington lobbyists[12]
☠ EC responsibility rating of POOR[30]
☠ *$12 billion* paid by taxpayers to bailout[54]

RESOURCES

www.fueleconomy.gov

CEREAL

A	A+	★Nature's Path, Envirokidz, ★Lydia's Organics
	A	Bob's Red Mill, Alvarado Street, Purely Elizabeth
	A−	Barbara's, Health Valley, Earth's Best, Lundberg, Arrowhead Mills
B	B+	Food For Life, Peace Cereal
	B	Cascadian Farm, General Mills, Kix, Pillsbury, Wheaties, Cheerios, Chex, Newman's Own, Total, Nature Valley
	B−	
C	C+	
	C	Quaker, Mother's, *Cream of Wheat*
	C−	Post, Grape Nuts, Shredded Wheat Weight Watchers, Malt-O-Meal, Heartland
D	D+	
	D	Kellogg's, Kashi, Corn Flakes, All-Bran, Frosted Flakes, Rice Crispies, Special K, Raisin Bran, Bear Naked
	D−	
F	F	☠ Back To Nature, Kraft, Nabisco, Nestlé

CEREAL

WHAT YOU NEED TO KNOW

Currently, choosing a socially responsible cereal is one of the easiest ways to make a difference with your dollars. You'll find many great choices available in most supermarkets.

GREEN HERO

Nature's Path

☆ GAM certified Green Business
☆ Named one of Canada's Greenest Employers
☆ Sponsors environmental efforts and festivals

GREEN HERO

Lydia's Organic

☆ GAM certified Green Business
☆ Does not test on animals
☆ Industry leader in organic integrity

CORPORATE VILLAIN

Back To Nature (Kraft)

☠ MM's "Worst Corporation" list for five years[51]
☠ Currently target of two major boycotts[22,55]
☠ Named global climate change laggard[15]

USEFUL RESOURCES

💻 www.cornucopia.org/cereal-scorecard

CHIPS

A	A+	★Eden Foods
	A	
	A–	Barbara's, Little Bear, Hain, Terra, Lundberg, Bearitos, Garden of Eatin'
B	B+	
	B	Food Should Taste Good
	B–	
C	C+	Stacy's
	C	Lay's, Cheetos, Doritos, Fritos, Sun Chips, Tostitos, Ruffles, Funyuns, Quaker, Pepperidge Farm, Mission, Kettle Chips, *True North, Cape Cod, Solea, Dirty's, Glicks, Utz, Hawaiian, Eat Smart, Boulder, Robert's American Gourmet, Genisoy,*
	C–	
D	D+	
	D	Pringles, French's
	D–	☠ Alexia
F	F	☠ Nabisco

CHIPS

BUYING TIPS

✓ Look for chips made with organic ingredients
✓ Avoid hydrogenated, saturated, and trans fats
✓ Buy larger quantities to reduce packaging

GREEN HERO

Eden Foods

☆ Ranked #18 best company on the planet
☆ CEP's highest social responsibility score
☆ GAM certified Green Business

CORPORATE VILLAIN

Nabisco (Kraft)

☠ Greenwash Award for public deception[25]
☠ Named global climate change laggard[15]
☠ Currently target of two major boycotts[22,55]
☠ Paid $329 million to Washington lobbyists[12]

CORPORATE VILLAIN

Alexia (ConAgra)

☠ MM's "Worst Corporation" list for two years[51]
☠ #50 in "Top 100 Corporate Criminals"[51]
☠ Ceres "Climate Change Laggard"[15]

USEFUL RESOURCES

💻 www.responsibleshopper.org

CHOCOLATE

A	**A+**	★Equal Exchange, Divine, Alter Eco, SweetRiot, Theo
	A	Shaman, Sjaak's, Coco-Zen, Endangered Species
	A–	Rapunzel
B	**B+**	Ah!Laska, Terra Nostra, Cloud Nine, Tropical Source, Sunspire, Lake Champlain
	B	Green & Black's, Newman's Own, Dagoba
	B–	
C	**C+**	Chocolove, Lindt, Ghirardelli
	C	*Nutella, Ferrero Rocher, Droste, Russell Stover, Whitman's, Ritter*
	C–	Godiva
D	**D+**	
	D	
	D–	Hershey's, Swiss Miss, Scharffen Berger
F	**F**	☠ Crunch, Wonka, Nestlé, Perugina, Toblerone, Mars, Ovaltine, Cadbury, Dove, M&M

CHOCOLATE

WHAT YOU NEED TO KNOW

Recently, the ILO, UNICEF, and US State Department uncovered the widespread use of child slave labor in the chocolate industry — up to 40% of all chocolate is currently being produced in this way.

BUYING TIPS

✓ Companies in the A category are slave-free
✓ Look for chocolate that is fair trade certified
✓ Buy organic chocolate when available

GREEN HERO

Equal Exchange

☆ GAM certified Green Business
☆ Business Ethics Award winner
☆ Industry leader in fair trade movement
☆ 4x Awarded "Most Democratic Workplace"

CORPORATE VILLAIN

Crunch (Nestlé)

☠ Aggressive takeovers of family farms[61]
☠ "Most Irresponsible" corporation award[6]
☠ Involved in child slavery lawsuit[61]

USEFUL RESOURCES

www.greenamerica.org

CLEANING PRODUCTS

A	A+	★Ecover, Method, Dr. Bronners, ★Seventh Generation, Biokleen
	A	Planet, Air Therapy, ECOS, Citra-Solv, Mountain Green, EcoLogic
	A–	Mrs. Meyers
B	B+	
	B	WD-40, Murphy's Oil, Ajax
	B–	Shaklee, Mr. Bubble, SC Johnson, Windex, Ziploc, Pledge, Fantastik, Drano, Bon Ami, Glade, Vanish
C	C+	
	C	*Hefty, Reynolds, Comet*
	C–	
D	D+	3M
	D	Amway, Lysol, Easy-Off, Wizard, Chore Boy, Resolve, Woolite, Reckitt Benckiser, Arm & Hammer
	D–	Soft Scrub, 20 Mule Team, Clorox, Green Works, Pine Sol, Tilex, Glad, Liquid-Plumr, Dial, SOS
F	F	☠ Swiffer, Procter & Gamble, Joy, Gain, Mr. Clean, Dawn, Febreze, Ivory, Sara Lee, Endust, Ty-D-Bol

CLEANING PRODUCTS

BUYING TIPS

✓ Look for non-petroleum based products
✓ Avoid products with chlorine/toxic chemicals

GREEN HERO

Seventh Generation

☆ #2 best company on the planet
☆ Empowers consumers w/packaging
☆ Winner, Sustainability Report Award
☆ Socially Responsible Business Award

GREEN HERO

Ecover

☆ GAM certified Green Business
☆ Winner, Environmental Leader Award
☆ UN Global 500 Environment Honor Roll
☆ 1st truly ecological factory in the world

CORPORATE VILLAIN

Swiffer (Procter & Gamble)

☠ MM's "Worst Corporation" list for two years[51]
☠ Continues unnecessary animal testing[10]
☠ "Bottom Rung," Ladder of Responsibility[40]
☠ Spent over $68 million on lobbyists[12]

CLOTHING

A	A+	★Maggie's Organics, Patagonia, Eileen Fisher, Alta Gracia
	A	No Enemy, Hempy's
	A−	Timberland, Nau
B	B+	GAP, Levi's
	B	Liz Claiborne, Nordstrom, H&M
	B−	Eddie Bauer, LL Bean
C	C+	Burberry, Billabong, Hanes, Coach, American Eagle, Britannia, Nicole Miller, Champion, Playtex
	C	Gucci, Tommy Hilfiger, Hugo Boss, Bass, Izod, Calvin Klein, J Crew, PVH, Armani, Under Armor, Diesel
	C−	Men's Warehouse, Christian Dior
D	D+	Abercrombie, Forever 21, Lands End
	D	Ross, DKNY, Target, Bill Blass, Lord & Taylor, Kohl's, JC Penney
	D−	Express, Limited, Victoria's Secret, TJ Maxx, Marshall's, Vanity Fair
F	F	☠ Macy's, Fruit of the Loom, Sears, Walmart, Sam's Club, Ralph Lauren, Dillard's, Kmart, Marshall Fields, Foley's, The North Face

CLOTHING

WHAT YOU NEED TO KNOW

The fact is that many of the clothes we wear today are made in sweatshops in the developing world. Better companies have either US-made clothing or strictly enforced human rights standards that ensure fair wages and safe working conditions.

GREEN HERO

Maggie's Organics

☆ Socially Responsible Business Award
☆ Industry leader in fair trade movement
☆ GAM "Top Rung," Ladder of Responsibility
☆ GAM certified Green Business

CORPORATE VILLAIN

Macy's

☠ Weak code of conduct for sweatshops[14]
☠ RS "F" for overall social responsibility[61]
☠ Named "Sweatshop Laggard" by CEP[14]
☠ "Bottom Rung," Ladder of Responsibility[40]

USEFUL RESOURCES

💻 www.cleanclothes.org
💻 en.maquilasolidarity.org
💻 www.free2work.org
💻 www.labourbehindthelabel.org

COFFEE

A	**A+**	★Equal Exchange, Alter Eco, Dean's Beans, Cafe Campesino, Grounds For Change, Moka Joe, Pura Vida, Peace Coffee, Higher Grounds
	A	Thanksgiving, Café Mam, Caffe Ibis, Larry's Beans, Jim's Organic, Elan, Pax Organica, Sustainable Harvest
	A–	LOCAL COFFEE SHOPS
B	**B+**	
	B	Starbucks, Green Mountain, K-Cup, Keurig, Newman's Own
	B–	illy, Alterra
C	**C+**	Peet's, Caribou
	C	Seattle's Best
	C–	LaVazza, Eight O'Clock
D	**D+**	
	D	Land O'Lakes
	D–	International Delight
F	**F**	☠ Nespresso, Sanka, Yuban, Nestlé, General Foods, Folgers, Maxwell House, Gevalia, CoffeeMate, Continental, Hill Bros, Nescafe

COFFEE

WHAT YOU NEED TO KNOW

Global coffee prices have plummeted recently, pushing some coffee farmers in the developing world to the brink of starvation. Buying fair trade coffee is now more important than ever.

BUYING TIPS

✓ Look for fair trade, shade grown, organic
✓ Support local, independent coffee shops

GREEN HERO

Equal Exchange

☆ 4x Awarded "Most Democratic Workplace"
☆ Worker-owned cooperative
☆ B Lab & GAM Certified Responsible Company
☆ Industry leader in fair trade movement
☆ Fair trade, organic, shade grown coffee

CORPORATE VILLAIN

Nespresso (Nestlé)

☠ Involved in union busting outside US[61]
☠ "Bottom Rung," Ladder of Responsibility[40]
☠ Aggressive takeovers of family farms[61]
☠ Baby formula human rights boycott[48]

USEFUL RESOURCES

www.transfairusa.org

COMPUTERS & ACCESSORIES

A	A+	
	A	
	A–	★HP, Cisco
B	B+	Google, Apple, Dell, Intel
	B	Canon, Adobe, AMD, Lucent
	B–	IBM, NEC, Lexmark, Symantec
C	C+	Seagate, Avaya, Logitech
	C	Sony, Brother, Novell, Oki, SanDisk, 3COM, Plantronics, Epson, Best Buy, Toshiba, Motorola, Western Digital, Asus, *Kensington, Fellowes*
	C–	McAfee, Sanyo, Maxell, Belkin, LSI, NCR, Micron, Fujitsu, LG
D	D+	JVC, Viewsonic, Gateway, Lenovo
	D	Samsung, Acer, AST, Hitachi, Sharp, Philips, Panasonic
	D–	Oracle, Peoplesoft
F	F	☠ Microsoft, GE

COMPUTERS & ACCESSORIES

WHAT YOU NEED TO KNOW

Computers have become an essential part of everyday life for many of us, but that need to stay up to date has also led to a rapidly growing problem of toxic computer waste in our landfills.

GREEN HERO

HP (Hewlett Packard)

- ☆ Free return recycling of its computers
- ☆ Perfect 100 on HRC Equality Index
- ☆ Countless awards for business ethics

CORPORATE VILLAIN

Microsoft

- ☠ RS "F" for overall social responsibility[40]
- ☠ Named "abusive monopoly" by US Court[48]
- ☠ Paid $150 million to Washington lobbyists[12]
- ☠ Greenpeace "Green Electronics Laggard"[44]
- ☠ Refuses disclosure on its business[14]

USEFUL RESOURCES

- www.greenpeace.org/greenerelectronics
- www.electronicstakeback.com
- www.svtc.org

CONDIMENTS & DRESSINGS

A	**A+**	★Eden Foods
	A	★Sierra Nevada, Annie's Naturals, San-J
	A–	Follow Your Heart, Vegenaise, Hain, Hollywood, Westbrae, Spectrum
B	**B+**	Ginger People, Nasoya, Woodstock Farms, OrganicVille, Bragg
	B	Muir Glen, Newman's Own
	B–	
C	**C+**	
	C	Pepperidge Farms, Mrs. Dash, *Wish-Bone, Tapatio, abasco, Sriracha*
	C–	Kikkoman, Thai Kitchen
D	**D+**	
	D	McCormick, Lawry's, Contadina, Del Monte, French's, La Victoria, Jack Daniel's, Heinz, Lea & Perrins, TGI Friday's, Best Foods, Lizano, Knorr
	D–	Hidden Valley, KC Masterpiece, La Choy, Gulden's, Hunt's
F	**F**	☠ Miracle Whip, Kraft, Bull's Eye, Grey Poupon, Good Seasons, A1

CONDIMENTS & DRESSINGS

WHAT YOU NEED TO KNOW

Whether you're looking for ketchup, mustard, mayonnaise, soy sauce, or salad dressing, there are now socially responsible brands of each.

BUYING TIPS

✓ Choose organic condiments when available

GREEN HERO

Eden Foods

☆ Ranked #18 best company on the planet
☆ CEP's highest social responsibility score
☆ Top rated for its organic integrity

GREEN HERO

Sierra Nevada

☆ Designated Climate Action Leader
☆ Numerous environmental awards
☆ Recycles 98% of waste created in production

CORPORATE VILLAIN

Miracle Whip (Kraft)

☠ Named "Top 10 Greenwasher"[48]
☠ Paid $329 million to Washington lobbyists[12]
☠ Involved in document deletion cover-up[48]

COOKIES & CRACKERS

A	A+	★Nature's Path, ★Lydia's Organic, Mary's Gone Crackers
	A	San-J, Annie's Naturals
	A–	Barbara's, Late July, Edward & Sons, Alternative Baking Co., Sun Flour Baking Co., Nature's Choice, Doctor Kracker, Lundberg, Hain, Health Valley, Earth's Best
B	B+	Immaculate
	B	Newman's Own, Cascadian Farm
	B–	
C	C+	
	C	Quaker, Mother's, Pepperidge Farm, Mi-del , *Pamela's, LU, Archway, Mrs. Fields, Manishewitz, Ryvita, Wasa*
	C–	Ry Krisp
D	D+	
	D	Keebler, Kashi, Famous Amos, Kellogg's, Sunshine
	D–	
F	F	☠ Nabisco, Back To Nature, Snackwell's, Red Oval

COOKIES & CRACKERS

WHAT YOU NEED TO KNOW

The socially responsible cookie industry has recently exploded, so there's no longer any need to feel guilty about reaching into the cookie jar.

GREEN HERO

Nature's Path

☆ GAM certified Green Business
☆ Named one of Canada's Greenest Employers
☆ Sponsors environmental efforts and festivals

GREEN HERO

Lydia's Organic

☆ GAM certified Green Business
☆ Does not test on animals
☆ Industry leader in organic integrity

CORPORATE VILLAIN

Nabisco (Kraft)

☠ Part of #2 worst company on the earth[10]
☠ Currently the target of 2 major boycotts[22,55]
☠ Spent over $329 million on lobbyists[12]
☠ Greenwash Award for public deception[48]

COSMETICS

A	**A+**	★EO, Tweezerman, ECO Lips, Pangea Organics, Aubrey Organics
	A	Aveda, Zia, Kiss My Face, Colorganics, Herbs of Grace
	A–	Dr. Hauschka, Weleda
B	**B+**	Lush, BWC
	B	Body Shop, Ecco Bella, Avon, Zuzu, Gabriel
	B–	Physician's Formula, CO Bigelow,
C	**C+**	Desert Essence, Burt's Bees, Nature's Gate
	C	Avalon Organics, *Sally Hansen, Wet & Wild, Cutex, Bare Escentuals, La Cross*
	C–	L'Oreal, Maybelline, Nivea, Sephora
D	**D+**	
	D	Melaleuca, Pond's, Mary Kay, Dove, Vaseline
	D–	Revlon, Almay, Neutrogena, Aveeno, Johnson & Johnson, Estee Lauder, Clinique
F	**F**	☠ CoverGirl, Max Factor, Oil of Olay, Noxema

COSMETICS

WHAT YOU NEED TO KNOW

While some cosmetics companies still carry out tests on animals, many smaller companies now provide animal- and eco-friendly alternatives.

BUYING TIPS

✓ Choose companies that don't test on animals
✓ Look for products with organic ingredients

GREEN HERO

EO

☆ Products never tested on animals
☆ GAM certified Green Business
☆ B Lab Certified Responsible Company
☆ Containers made from recycled PET bottles

CORPORATE VILLAIN

CoverGirl (Procter & Gamble)

☠ Continues unnecessary animal testing[10]
☠ "Bottom Rung," Ladder of Responsibility[40]
☠ MM's "Worst Corporation" list for two years[51]
☠ Spent over $68 million on lobbyists[12]

USEFUL RESOURCES

💻 www.caringconsumer.org
💻 www.ewg.org

DAIRY ALTERNATIVES

A	A+	★Organic Valley, ★Nancy's, Eden, Wildwood, WholeSoy, Hemp Bliss
	A	So Delicious
	A–	Stonyfield Farm, Follow Your Heart, WestSoy
B	B+	Good Karma
	B	Earth/Smart Balance, ZenSoy, Pacific
	B–	Silk, Soya Kaas, Vitasoy
C	C+	
	C	Tofutti, *Lisanatti, Soy Moon, Califia, Soyco, Soymage, Veggie/Rice Slice, Blue Diamond, Almond Breeze*
	C–	Soy/Rice/Almond Dream, Go Veggie!, 8th Continent
D	D+	
	D	
	D–	International Delight
F	F	☠ Cool Whip, Carnation

DAIRY ALTERNATIVES

BUYING TIPS

✓ Choose organic products when available
✓ Look for items with easily recycled containers

GREEN HERO

Organic Valley

☆ Largest US cooperative of small, family farms
☆ Top rated for its organic integrity
☆ Multiple responsible business awards

GREEN HERO

Nancy's

☆ Largely solar powered workplace
☆ GAM certified Green Business
☆ 2x Socially Responsible Business Awards

CORPORATE VILLAIN

Cool Whip (Kraft)

☠ Currently target of two major boycotts[22,55]
☠ #3 contributor to Washington lobbyists[12]
☠ Involved in document deletion cover-up[48]

USEFUL RESOURCES

💻 www.organicconsumers.org
💻 www.cornucopia.org/soysurvey

DAIRY PRODUCTS

A	A+	★Organic Valley, Nancy's, Organic Pastures, Straus Family Creamery, Redwood Hill Farm
	A	Helios
	A–	Stonyfield Farm, Brown Cow, Cabot
B	B+	Lifeway
	B	Wallaby, Clover Stornetta, Yoplait, Dannon
	B–	
C	C+	
	C	Horizon, Kerrygold, *Daisy, Sargento, Alpine Lace, Chavrie, Mountain High, President, Rondele, Alouette, Hood, Athenos, Precious, Pavel's, Crystal, Tillamook*
	C–	Weight Watchers
D	D+	
	D	Sara Lee, Continental, Land O' Lakes, Kozy Shack, Laughing Cow
	D–	Hunt's, Reddi-Wip, Borden, Lactaid, Alta Dena
F	F	☠ Cracker Barrel, Jell-O, Nestlé, Knudsen, Back to Nature, Velveeta, Philadephia Cream Cheese, Kraft

DAIRY PRODUCTS

WHAT YOU NEED TO KNOW

While large corporate farms are the norm for the dairy industry, many small, family farms are fighting back by going organic in order to survive.

BUYING TIPS

✓ Look for "No Hormones" and "No Antibiotics"
✓ Choose items made with organic ingredients

GREEN HERO

Organic Valley

☆ Largest US cooperative of small, family farms
☆ Top rated for its organic integrity
☆ Multiple responsible business awards

CORPORATE VILLAIN

Cracker Barrel (Kraft)

☠ Part of #2 worst company on the earth[4]
☠ Currently the target of 2 major boycotts[22,55]
☠ Greenwashing Award for public deception[18]
☠ Named global climate change laggard[15]
☠ Named "Top 10 Greenwasher"[48]

USEFUL RESOURCES

- www.organicconsumers.org
- www.cornucopia.org/dairy_brand_ratings

DENTAL CARE

A	**A+**	★Preserve
	A	Kiss My Face, Auromere
	A–	Tom's of Maine, Xyliwhite, Jäsön, Weleda
B	**B+**	Ecodent, Radius, Natural Dentist, Fuchs, NOW
	B	Colgate, Ultrabrite
	B–	
C	**C+**	Nature's Gate, Burt's Bees
	C	*Desert Essence, GUM*
	C–	
D	**D+**	
	D	Arm & Hammer, Aim, Mentadent Pepsodent, Unilever
	D–	Johnson & Johnson, Rembrandt, Listerine, Reach
F	**F**	☠ Crest, Sensodyne, Scope, Oral-B, ☠ Aquafresh, Fixodent, Anbesol, ACT, GlaxoSmithKline, Polident, Poligrip, Abreva, Procter & Gamble

DENTAL CARE

WHAT YOU NEED TO KNOW

Smaller, environmentally friendly companies now offer increasingly popular alternatives to the dental products of larger, mainstream corporations.

BUYING TIPS

✓ Buy products made with recycled content
✓ Buy items with easily recycled packaging

GREEN HERO

Preserve (Recycline)

☆ Environmental leader in industry
☆ Products from 100% recycled plastic
☆ Take-back recycling of all products

CORPORATE VILLAIN

Crest (Procter & Gamble)

☠ GAM "Bottom Rung," responsibility rating[40]
☠ NRDC named "environmental laggard"[53]
☠ Paid $68 million to Washington lobbyists[12]

CORPORATE VILLAIN

Aquafresh (GlaxoSmithKline)

☠ MM's "Worst Corporation" list for two years[51]
☠ CEP "F" for overall social responsibility[14]
☠ Paid $86 million to Washington lobbyists[12]

EGGS

A	A+	★Pete & Gerry's, Organic Valley
	A	Vital Farms, Alexandre Kids, Lazy 69, Old Friends, Burroughs Family, Keedysville, Schultz, World's Best Eggs, St. John Family
	A–	
B	B+	Born Free, Egg Innovations, Wilcox, Stiebrs, Giving Nature, Farmers Hen House, Happy Egg, Giving Nature
	B	Clover Stornetta, Trader Joe's
	B–	
C	C+	Horizon Organic, 4 Grain, Sauder's, Country Hen
	C	Chino Valley, Glaum, Judy's Family Farm, Farmer's Harvest, Eggology, *Nulaid, Gold Circle*
	C–	
D	D+	Decoster
	D	Land O'Lakes, Eggland's Best, Lucerne
	D–	☠ Egg Beaters
F	F	

EGGS

WHAT YOU NEED TO KNOW

Factory farming has made egg production today a cruel and environmentally damaging endeavor. Seek out smaller, more humane options.

BUYING TIPS

✓ Look for cage-free or free-range eggs
✓ Buy organic eggs whenever possible
✓ Seek out local farmers markets

GREEN HERO

Pete & Gerry's

☆ B Lab Certified Responsible Company
☆ Supports sustainable, family farms
☆ First Certified Humane US egg producer

CORPORATE VILLAIN

EggBeaters (ConAgra)

☠ Involved in major accounting scandal[73]
☠ 2nd largest E. coli meat recall in history[55]
☠ Many worker safety & health violations[61]

USEFUL RESOURCES

💻 www.cornucopia.org/organic-egg-scorecard
💻 www.certifiedhumane.org

ELECTRONICS

A	**A+**	
	A	
	A–	
B	**B+**	★Apple
	B	Texas Instruments, Kodak, Canon
	B–	Norelco, Minolta, Konica, Conair
C	**C+**	Denon
	C	Toshiba, Garmin, Energizer, Haier, Eveready, Best Buy, Kenwood, Sony, Aiwa, Grundig, Pentax, Koss, Nikon, Rayovac, Plantronics, Sennheiser, Coby, *TDK, Apex, Magnavox, Tivo, Uniden*
	C–	Fujitsu, Polaroid, HTC, Bosch, LG, Sanyo, Maxell, Sylvania, Fuji, RCA, Fry's
D	**D+**	Olympus, Viewsonic, Radio Shack, JVC, 3M, Thomson
	D	Sharp, Philips, Daewoo, Hitachi, Samsung, Panasonic, Vizio
	D–	Amazon, Mitsubishi, Emerson
F	**F**	☠ GE, Duracell, Microsoft, Nintendo

ELECTRONICS

WHAT YOU NEED TO KNOW

Our addiction to the latest electronics has created a significant drain on our energy grid (even when they're off!) as well as a major recycling problem.

BUYING TIPS

✓ Look for electronics with Energy Star labels
✓ Buy rechargeable (NiMH) batteries
✓ Choose electronics that are recyclable

GREEN HERO

Apple

☆ Takes back iPods & computers for recycling
☆ All computers are Energy Star certified
☆ Perfect 100 on HRC Equality Index for nine years

CORPORATE VILLAIN

GE (General Electric)

☠ MM's "Worst Corporation" list for five years[51]
☠ Responsible for 116 toxic Superfund sites[61]
☠ #1 contributor to Washington lobbyists[12]
☠ #4 of PERI 100 Most Toxic Air Polluters[58]

USEFUL RESOURCES

💻 www.electronicstakeback.com
💻 www.svtc.org

ENERGY BARS

A	A+	★CLIF, Luna, Nutiva, Alpsnack, ★Nature's Path
	A	BumbleBar
	A–	Larabar, Think, Boomi, Health Valley
B	B+	ProBar, ReBAR, Raw Revolution, Crispy Cat
	B	Cascadian Farm, Nature Valley, General Mills
	B–	
C	C+	
	C	Quaker, Odwalla, *Kind, Atkins, Roman Meal, Soy Joy, Fit Smart, Promax, Met-Rx, Genisoy, Fubar, Sunbelt*
	C–	PowerBar
D	D+	
	D	Kellogg's, Kashi, Nutrigrain, Tiger's Milk, Slim Fast
	D–	
F	F	☠ Balance, South Beach, Kudos, Snickers, Kraft, Zone

ENERGY BARS

WHAT YOU NEED TO KNOW

Because many energy bar companies have truly stepped up to the plate, your choice of energy bar is one of the easiest ways to make a powerful difference for people and the planet.

GREEN HERO

CLIF

☆ Winner, Business Ethics Award
☆ EPA Green Power Leader award winner
☆ #12 best company on the earth

GREEN HERO

Nature's Path

☆ GAM certified Green Business
☆ Named one of Canada's Greenest Employers
☆ Sponsors environmental efforts and festivals

CORPORATE VILLAIN

Balance (Kraft)

☠ Part of #2 worst company on the earth[4]
☠ Named global climate change laggard[15]
☠ Named "Top 10 Greenwasher"[48]
☠ #3 top contributor to Washington lobbyists[12]

ENERGY DRINKS

A	A+	★Guayaki, CLIF, Adina
	A	Sambazon
	A–	Honest Tea, Bossa Nova, Zola, Steaz
B	B+	Hansen's, Blue Sky, Monster
	B	Starbucks
	B–	Recharge
C	C+	
	C	Gatorade, SoBe, MDX, Propel, AMP, Red Bull, *5-Hour Energy, FRS, Rip It, Bawls, Atkins, Go Girl, Muscle Milk, Guru, Fubar, Everlast, Met-Rx, Celsius, Xenergy*
	C–	Arizona, Jones, Rockstar
D	D+	Snapple
	D	Lipton, Slim Fast, Special K
	D–	
F	F	☠ Full Throttle, Boost, Fuze, Vault, Vitamin Water, Powerade, Tab, BPM, Glaceau, Ensure

ENERGY DRINKS

WHAT YOU NEED TO KNOW

Just in the past two years have socially responsible choices for energy drinks finally become available. It's important to support these options wherever you find them.

BUYING TIPS

✓ Buy drinks in aluminum or glass containers

GREEN HERO

Guayaki

☆ Organic, fair trade certified products
☆ Uses sustainably harvested, rainforest plants
☆ 3x Awarded "Most Democratic Workplace"
☆ GAM certified Green Business

CORPORATE VILLAIN

Full Throttle (Coca Cola)

☠ MM's "Worst Corporation" list for three years[51]
☠ CAI hinders clean water access abroad[22]
☠ Target of major human rights boycotts[30]
☠ Paid $73 million to Washington lobbyists[12]

USEFUL RESOURCES

- www.opensecrets.org
- www.stopcorporateabuse.org
- www.multinationalmonitor.org

FAST FOOD & RESTAURANTS

A	**A+**	
	A	★Chipotle, Burgerville, evos, Pizza Fusion, b.good, Boloco, Native Foods
	A–	LarkBurger, Le Pan Quotidien
B	**B+**	
	B	In-N-Out, Noodles & Co.
	B–	Bruegger's Bagels, Einstein Bros.
C	**C+**	Panera
	C	Boston Market, Chuck E Cheese, Ruby Tuesday's, Moe's, Shoney's
	C–	Red Robin, Popeye's, Papa John's, Quiznos, Panda Express, Chik-fil-A
D	**D+**	Subway, Chili's, TGI Fridays, Dunkin' Donuts
	D	Applebee's, Jack in the Box, Qdoba, Outback Steakhouse, Olive Garden, Buffalo Wild Wings, Red Lobster, Little Caesar's, Sonic, DQ, Denny's, Hardee's, Carl's Jr, IHOP, Domino's
	D–	Wendy's, Arby's, Cracker Barrel, Burger King, McDonald's
F	**F**	☠ KFC, Taco Bell, Pizza Hut, Long John Silver, Baja Fresh, A&W

FAST FOOD & RESTAURANTS

WHAT YOU NEED TO KNOW

The overall picture of the highly competitive fast food industry is not a pretty one, but if you find yourself in a pinch, there are a handful of companies to choose from that are on the cutting edge of responsibility. Support them whenever possible and let them know that you appreciate their efforts.

GREEN HERO

Chipotle

☆ Actively sources from family farms
☆ 40% of beans utilized are organic
☆ 70% of meat utilized is naturally raised

CORPORATE VILLAIN

KFC (Kentucky Fried Chicken)

☠ Linked to rainforest destruction abroad[44]
☠ Involved with plastic toy sweatshops[61]
☠ Target of major consumer boycott[30]
☠ Evidence of false nutritional claims[61]

USEFUL RESOURCES

💻 www.cspinet.org
💻 www.responsibleshopper.org

FEMININE CARE

A	A+	★Seventh Generation, Gladrags, ★Luna Pads
	A	The Keeper, Moon Cup, Diva Cup
	A–	Organic Essentials, Natracare, Maxim
B	B+	
	B	Kotex, Poise
	B–	
C	C+	
	C	Playtex, *Summer's Eve, EPT, Vagisil, Massengill*
	C–	
D	D+	
	D	First Response, Clearblue
	D–	Stayfree, O.B., Carefree
F	F	☠ Tampax, Always

FEMININE CARE

WHAT YOU NEED TO KNOW

Much of the effort for socially responsible business has been driven by women, so it's not surprising that there are many great options in this category.

BUYING TIPS

✓ Buy care products with less packaging waste

GREEN HERO

Seventh Generation

☆ Ranked #2 best company on the planet
☆ Empowers consumers w/packaging
☆ Socially Responsible Business Award

GREEN HERO

Luna Pads

☆ GAM certified Green Business
☆ B Lab Certified Responsible Company
☆ EC overall responsibility rating of GOOD

CORPORATE VILLAIN

Tampax (Procter & Gamble)

☠ MM's "Worst Corporation" list for two years[51]
☠ Continues unnecessary animal testing[10]
☠ Target of major consumer boycott[30]

FROZEN DINNERS

A	A+	
	A	★Amy's Kitchen, Annie's, Tofurky
	A–	Ethnic Gourmet, Rising Moon, Moosewood, Applegate Farms
B	B+	Linda McCartney
	B	Ian's, Totino's, Cascadian Farm, Newman's Own
	B–	
C	C+	Seeds of Change
	C	Swanson, Hungry Man, Birds Eye, Foster Farms, Van de Kamps, *Claim Jumper, Michelina's, Tony's, Michael Angelo's, Gorton's, Health Is Wealth, Ling Ling, Lean Gourmet, Freschetta, Red Baron*
	C–	Quorn, Weight Watchers
D	D+	
	D	Bertolli, TGI Friday's, Ore-Ida, Smart Ones, Boston Market, Bagel Bites, Kashi
	D–	Healthy Choice, Marie Callender's, Banquet, Alexia
F	F	☠ Lean Cuisine, Stouffer's, Boca, ☠ Uncle Ben's, Tyson, Hot Pockets

FROZEN DINNERS

WHAT YOU NEED TO KNOW

Today's stress-filled lifestyles have created increasing demand for quick and easy meals. Luckily, a number of responsible companies have decided to focus on options that are good for people and the planet.

GREEN HERO

Amy's Kitchen

- ☆ Donates food to relief efforts
- ☆ Produces all-vegetarian, organic foods
- ☆ GAM certified Green Business

CORPORATE VILLAIN

Lean Cuisine (Nestlé)

- ☠ Baby formula human rights boycott[48]
- ☠ "Most Irresponsible" corporation award[6]
- ☠ Aggressive takeovers of family farms[61]
- ☠ Involved in union busting outside US[61]

CORPORATE VILLAIN

Uncle Ben's (Mars)

- ☠ On MM's "10 Worst Corporations" list[51]
- ☠ Evidence of involvement in child slave labor[61]
- ☠ Target of international fair trade campaign[25]
- ☠ Paid $36 million to Washington lobbyists[12]

FRUIT & VEGETABLES

A	A+	LOCAL FARMERS MARKETS, CSAs, ★Equal Exchange
	A	Earthbound Farm
	A–	Olivia's, Stahlbush, Cal-Organic, Bunny Luv, Woodstock Farms, Grimmway Farms, Organic Girl
B	B+	HerbThyme, Pure Pacific
	B	Cascadian Farm, Newman's Own, Driscoll's, Ian's, Green Giant
	B–	Sunsweet, Sun-Maid
C	C+	
	C	Tropicana, *Birds Eye, Ready Pac, Salad Time, Flav-R-Pac, C&W*
	C–	Ocean Spray
D	D+	Sunkist
	D	Dole, Ore-Ida, Del Monte
	D–	☠ Fresh Express, Hidden Valley, Alexia
F	F	

FRUIT & VEGETABLES

WHAT YOU NEED TO KNOW

Fresh produce is the vanguard of the organic foods movement. It's particularly important to buy local produce, so attend your local farmers' market or join a CSA (community supported agriculture) farm.

GREEN HERO

Equal Exchange

☆ 4x Awarded "Most Democratic Workplace"
☆ Worker-owned cooperative
☆ B Lab & GAM Certified Responsible Company
☆ Industry leader in fair trade movement

CORPORATE VILLAIN

Fresh Express (Chiquita)

☠ MM's "Worst Corporation" list for two years[51]
☠ Hired Colombian criminals to protect crops[48]
☠ EC overall responsibility rating of POOR[30]
☠ Evaded taxes using offshore bank accounts[61]

USEFUL RESOURCES

💻 www.localharvest.org
💻 www.farmfresh.org

GASOLINE

A	A+	
	A	
	A–	
B	B+	
	B	★Sunoco
	B–	Petro Canada
C	C+	Citgo, Hess, Ultramar
	C	Circle K, Costco, *Sinclair, Husky, Mohawk, Irving, Rutter's, Astro, Murphy, Pioneer, QuickChek, Wawa, Tesoro, QuikTrip, RaceTrac, Zephyr*
	C–	Total, Valero, Beacon, Diamond Shamrock, Stop N Go
D	D+	Marathon, Ashland, Speedway, Pilot, SuperAmerica, Flying J
	D	Conoco, Phillips 66, Jet, Superclean Tosco, Union 76
	D–	Shell, BP, Arco
F	F	☠ Exxon, Mobil, Esso, Chevron, Gulf, Texaco, Unocal

GASOLINE

WHAT YOU NEED TO KNOW

The petroleum industry is one of the least socially and environmentally responsible on the planet, so if you don't want to get your hands dirty, you should sell your car. For the rest of us, it's very important to avoid the companies at the bottom of this category as they are some of the most destructive in existence.

BUYING TIPS

✓ Locate the best ranked gas station near your home and work

GREEN HERO

Sunoco

☆ Most eco-friendly refineries in industry
☆ Only oil signatory to CERES Principles
☆ 1st company to recognize climate change

CORPORATE VILLAIN

Exxon-Mobil

☠ #1 worst corporation on the planet[4]
☠ Repeated violator of human rights[61]
☠ #5 in "Top 100 Corporate Criminals"[51]
☠ Paid $247 million to Washington lobbyists[12]
☠ Only negative score ever given by HRC[46]
☠ Extensive record of environmental damage[48]

HAIR CARE

A	A+	★Druide, EO, Dr. Bronner's, Aubrey
	A	Aveda, Kiss My Face
	A–	Weleda, Tom's of Maine, Jäsön, Alba
B	B+	BWC
	B	Body Shop, Lush, Ecco Bella, Pure & Basic, Citre Shine, Shikai, Pureology, Paul Mitchell, Paul Penders
	B–	
C	C+	Burt's Bees, Nature's Gate
	C	Avalon Organics, Giovanni, Desert Essence, *Dep, Biosilk, AquaNet, Prell, Matrix, Joico, Crew, Finesse, Biolage*
	C–	L'Oréal
D	D+	
	D	Dove, Suave, Axe, SunSilk, Nexxus, Tresemme, VO5, St. Ives
	D–	☠ Revlon, Neutrogena, Aveeno, Purell, Rogaine
F	F	☠ Clairol, Aussie, Head & Shoulders, Herbal Essences, Vidal Sassoon, Pert, Pantene, Ivory, Selsun Blue

HAIR CARE

BUYING TIPS

✓ Avoid products tested on animals
✓ Seek out items made with organic ingredients
✓ Buy recyclable containers: #1, #2 plastic
✓ Buy larger quantities to reduce packaging

GREEN HERO

Druide

☆ 100% sustainably harvested ingredients
☆ Uses strict ECOCERT organic standards
☆ Fair trade, organic ingredients
☆ Industry leader in environment category

CORPORATE VILLAIN

Clairol (Proctor & Gamble)

☠ Continues unnecessary animal testing[10]
☠ GAM "Bottom Rung," responsibility rating[40]
☠ NRDC named "environmental laggard"[53]
☠ Paid $68 million to Washington lobbyists[12]

CORPORATE VILLAIN

Revlon

☠ CEP "F" for overall social responsibility[14]
☠ Continues unnecessary animal testing[10]
☠ Refuses disclosure to consumers[14]

HOTELS

A	A+	★Kimpton Hotels
	A	Couchsurfing International
	A–	
B	B+	
	B	Marriott, Courtyard, Ritz Carlton, Renaissance, Bulgari, Saunders
	B–	Hyatt, Wyndham, Ramada, Super 8, Days Inn, Howard Johnson, Motel 6, Novotel, Sofitel, Red Roof Inn, Westin
C	C+	Knights Inn, Hawthorn, Harrah's, Comfort Inn/Suites, Econo Lodge, Quality Inn, Clarion
	C	Best Western, Radisson, Hotels.com, *La Quinta Inn*
	C–	Sheraton, Westin, Starwood, Crowne Plaza, Express, Holiday Inn, MGM, Carlson, Travelodge, Express
D	D+	
	D	☠ Hilton, Hampton Inn, DoubleTree, Conrad, Embassy
	D–	
F	F	

HOTELS

WHAT YOU NEED TO KNOW

Whether for business or pleasure, choosing where you stay can have a greater impact than even how you travel there and back.

BUYING TIPS

✓ Whenever possible, stay in a locally owned inn, bed & breakfast, or international hostel.

GREEN HERO

Kimpton Hotels

- ☆ Environmental leader in the hotel industry
- ☆ Perfect 100 on HRC Equality Index
- ☆ Green Seal certified green lodging
- ☆ GAM certified Green Business

CORPORATE VILLAIN

Hilton Hotels

- ☠ Rated "Very Poor" by Ethical Consumer[30]
- ☠ CC foot dragging on climate change efforts[30]
- ☠ Paid $55 million to Washington lobbyists[12]

USEFUL RESOURCES

- www.greenhotels.com
- www.sustainabletravel.org
- www.tripadvisor.com/GreenLeaders

ICE CREAM & FROZEN DESSERTS

A	A+	★Straus Family, Wholesoy
	A	Amy's Kitchen, Sambazon, So Delicious, Purely Decadent
	A–	Ben & Jerry's, Stonyfield Farm, Alden's, Julie's Organic, Cabot, Ciao Bella, Coconut Bliss, Three Twins
B	B+	FrutStix, Wholly Wholesome, Tru Whip, Ah!Laska,
	B	Starbucks, Newman's Own, Pillsbury
	B–	
C	C+	
	C	Pepperidge Farm, Tofutti, Dr.Oetker
	C–	Almond/Rice/Soy Dream, Godiva
D	D+	
	D	Klondike, Breyers, Good Humor
	D–	Marie Callender's, Reddi-wip, Hershey's
F	F	☠ Dreyer's, Eskimo Pie, Nestlé, ☠ Snickers, Edy's, Häagen Dazs, Skinny Cow, Kraft, Cool Whip, Sara Lee, Dove, Jell-O

ICE CREAM & FROZEN DESSERTS

BUYING TIPS

✓ Choose ice cream with organic ingredients
✓ Look for fair trade coffee/chocolate flavors

GREEN HERO

Straus Family

☆ 1st 100% organic dairy in US
☆ Uses returnable glass bottles for milk
☆ Utilizes methane capture for waste
☆ Small, sustainable family farm

CORPORATE VILLAIN

Dreyer's (Nestlé)

☠ Baby formula human rights boycott[48]
☠ "Most Irresponsible" corporation award[6]
☠ Involved in child slavery lawsuit[61]
☠ Aggressive takeovers of family farms[61]

CORPORATE VILLAIN

Snickers (Mars)

☠ On MM's "10 Worst Corporations" list[51]
☠ Evidence of involvement in child slave labor[61]
☠ Target of international fair trade campaign[25]
☠ Paid $36 million to Washington lobbyists[12]

INSURANCE COMPANIES

A	A+	★Better World Club
	A	
	A–	
B	B+	
	B	Kaiser Permanente
	B–	Chubb, Progressive, Nationwide, TIAA-CREF
C	C+	Principal Financial
	C	Cigna, Esurance, Travelers, Pacific Life, UnumProvident, USAA, AAA, Amica, Humana, Mutual of Omaha, Capital One, Safeco
	C–	American Family, Humana, Aetna
D	D+	United Healthcare, MetLife, Allstate
	D	GEICO, Farmers, Mass Mutual, Northwestern Mutual, New York Life, AFLAC, State Farm
	D–	Prudential, Berkshire Hathaway, Liberty Mutual
F	F	☠ AIG, ☠ Blue Cross / Blue Shield

INSURANCE COMPANIES

WHAT YOU NEED TO KNOW

Whether for our car, health, home, or life, most of us need to buy insurance sooner or later. As we've discovered with the recent corporate bailouts, who we choose to do business with can have serious implications for our personal and national pocketbooks.

GREEN HERO

Better World Club

- ☆ Social Venture Network member
- ☆ GAM certified Green Business
- ☆ Only insurance signatory to CERES Principles

CORPORATE VILLAIN

AIG (American International Group)

- ☠ MM's "Worst Corporation" list for two years[51]
- ☠ Paid $82 million to Washington lobbyists[12]
- ☠ $170 *billion* paid by taxpayers to bailout[54]

CORPORATE VILLAIN

Blue Cross / Blue Shield

- ☠ #41 in "Top 100 Corporate Criminals"[51]
- ☠ RS "F" for overall social responsibility[61]
- ☠ Paid $303 million to Washington lobbyists[12]

JUICE

A	A+	★Organic Valley, Adina
	A	Sambazon, Kombucha Botanica
	A–	Purity, Columbia Gorge, Zola, Happy Planet, Apple & Eve, Lakewood, Mountain Sun
B	B+	Santa Cruz Organic, Ginger People, Hansen's
	B	Newman's Own, Cascadian Farm, Naked Juice
	B–	Florida's Natural
C	C+	Biotta, Horizon
	C	TreeTop, Tropicana, Gatorade, Odwalla, Welch's, Martinelli's, POM, Langers, V8, Campbell's
	C–	Jamba Juice, Kern's, RW Knudsen, Ocean Spray
D	D+	ReaLemon, Snapple, Del Monte, Mott's, Sunkist
	D	Dole, Sunny Delight
	D–	
F	F	☠ Minute Maid, Capri Sun, Libby's, ☠ Back to Nature, Crystal Light, Simply Orange, Kool-Aid, Hawaiian Punch, Juicy Juice

JUICE

BUYING TIPS

✓ Purchase organic juices when available
✓ Buy juices in aluminum or glass containers
✓ #1 or #2 when plastics are the only option
✓ Buy larger quantities to reduce packaging

GREEN HERO

Organic Valley

☆ Small family farmer-owned co-operative
☆ Gives 10% of profits to local community
☆ Humane animal treatment a priority
☆ Ranked #3 best company on the planet

CORPORATE VILLAIN

Minute Maid (Coca Cola)

☠ MM's "Worst Corporation" list for 3 years[51]
☠ Hinders clean water access abroad[22]
☠ Target of major human rights boycotts[30]

CORPORATE VILLAIN

Back to Nature (Kraft)

☠ Greenwash Award for public deception[48]
☠ MM's "Worst Corporation" list for five years[51]
☠ Named global climate change laggard[15]
☠ Paid $329 million to Washington lobbyists[12]

LAUNDRY SUPPLIES

A	A+	★Ecover, Method, Biokleen, Seventh Generation, Earth Friendly
	A	Planet, Mountain Green, ECOS, OxoBrite, Citra Solv
	A–	Mrs. Meyers, Country Save, Bio Pac
B	B+	Lifetree
	B	Dynamo, Spot Shot, Spree, Fab, Hurricane, Cold Power, Suavitel
	B–	Shout, Shaklee
C	C+	
	C	*Fresh Start, All, Wisk, Sunlight, Surf, Snuggle, Cuddlesoft, Sun*
	C–	
D	D+	
	D	Arm & Hammer, Oxi Clean, Xtra, Static Guard, Woolite, Calgon, Cling Free, Spray'n Wash
	D–	Clorox, Purex, 20 Mule Team Borax, Green Works
F	F	☠ Tide, Cheer, Biz, Bold, Gain, Dreft, Downy, Bounce, Era, Ivory, Febreze

LAUNDRY SUPPLIES

BUYING TIPS

✓ Avoid #3 plastic containers
✓ Choose #1 or #2 plastic when needed
✓ Avoid phosphates and chlorine bleach

GREEN HERO

Ecover

☆ GAM certified Green Business
☆ Winner, environmental leader award
☆ UN Global 500 Environment Honor Roll
☆ Named 1st sustainable factory in the world

CORPORATE VILLAIN

Tide (Procter & Gamble)

☠ Continues unnecessary animal testing[10]
☠ MM's "Worst Corporation" list for two years[51]
☠ GAM "Bottom Rung," responsibility rating[40]
☠ NRDC named "environmental laggard"[53]
☠ Paid $68 million to Washington lobbyists[12]

USEFUL RESOURCES

- www.greenamerica.org/livinggreen
- www.epa.gov/epp/pubs/cleaning.htm
- www.ewg.org/guides/cleaners
- www.ecocycle.org

MEAT ALTERNATIVES

A	A+	
	A	★Tofurky, Amy's Kitchen, Local Tofu, Fantastic Foods, Sunshine Burgers, Turtle Island, Wildwood
	A–	Small Planet, FarmSoy, Vermont Soy, Green Cuisine, Unisoy, Yves, TofuTown, Twin Oaks
B	B+	Nasoya, SoyBoy, Tofu Shop, Fresh Tofu, Sunergia, Central Soyfoods, Field Roast
	B	Ian's
	B–	White Wave, Vitasoy, Pete's, O'Soy
C	C+	
	C	Soy Deli, *Veat, Veggie Patch, Health Is Wealth, Sweet Earth, Primal Strips*
	C–	Quorn, Mori-Nu, Full Circle
D	D+	
	D	Morningstar, Gardenburger
	D–	Lightlife
F	F	☠ Boca Burgers

MEAT ALTERNATIVES

WHAT YOU NEED TO KNOW

Meat alternatives have come a long way since the days of tofu jokes. Burgers, hot dogs, chicken strips, lunch meat, and more are now convincingly tasty in vegetarian form and tend to have a smaller ecological footprint than their counterparts.

GREEN HERO

Tofurky (Turtle Island)

- ☆ EPA Certified 100% Green Power
- ☆ Highest standards of organic integrity
- ☆ 1st food sponsor of the Humane Society

CORPORATE VILLAIN

Boca Burgers (Kraft)

- ☠ Greenwash Award for public deception[48]
- ☠ MM's "Worst Corporation" list for five years[51]
- ☠ Named global climate change laggard[15]
- ☠ Paid $329 million to Washington lobbyists[12]

USEFUL RESOURCES

- 💻 www.cornucopia.org/soysurvey
- 💻 www.organicconsumers.org

MEAT PRODUCTS

A	A+	★Organic Prairie
	A	Green Zabiha
	A–	Niman Ranch, Diestel, Applegate Farms, Five Dot Ranch, Eel River, Shelton's, MBA Brand, Coleman
B	B+	
	B	
	B–	
C	C+	
	C	Foster Farms, *Armour, Empire Kosher, Valley Fresh, Saag's, Hickory Farms, Underwood*
	C–	
D	D+	Perdue
	D	Hormel, SPAM, Dinty Moore, Farmer John, Jennie-O, Stagg
	D–	Slim Jim, Hebrew National, Banquet, Healthy Choice, Butterball
F	F	☠ Ball Park Franks, Tyson, Jimmy Dean, Hillshire Farm, Oscar Mayer, Louis Rich, Smithfield, Farmland, Eckrich, Premium Standard, Cook's, Libby's

MEAT PRODUCTS

WHAT YOU NEED TO KNOW

Meat production tends to consume more resources than agriculture, so it's especially important to choose sustainable, humane options.

BUYING TIPS

✓ Choose free-range, organic meat options

GREEN HERO

Organic Prairie (Organic Valley)

☆ Small, family farmer cooperative
☆ Gives 10% of profits to local community
☆ Humane animal treatment a priority

CORPORATE VILLAIN

Ball Park Franks (Tyson)

☠ MM's "Worst Corporation" list for two years[51]
☠ CEP "F" for overall social responsibility[14]
☠ Guilty of 20+ violations of Clean Air Act[61]
☠ #52 in "Top 100 Corporate Criminals"[51]

USEFUL RESOURCES

💻 www.humanesociety.org
💻 www.organicconsumers.org
💻 www.certifiedhumane.org

MEDICAL

A	A+	★Traditional Medicinals
	A	
	A–	Nature's Way
B	B+	Ricola
	B	Medtronic
	B–	
C	C+	Baxter Intl.
	C	Biovail, Del
	C–	Novo Nordisk, Genentech
D	D+	3M, Bausch & Lomb, DaVita
	D	PhRMA, Reckitt Benckiser, Unilever, Tyco, Bristol-Myers Squibb, WR Grace, AstraZeneca, Mead Johnson
	D–	Sanofi, Merck, Motrin, Band-Aid, Benadryl, Tylenol, Neosporin, Eli Lilly, Johnson & Johnson, Schering-Plough, Dr. Scholl, McNeil, Rolaids, Visine,
F	F	☠ Pfizer, Halls, Merial, Cortizone, Gold Bond, IcyHot, Allegra, Unisom, Pharmacia, Abbott, Merck, Pamprin, Day/Nyquil, Novartis, Advil, Pepto-Bismol, Metamucil, Vick's, Procter & Gamble, Bayer, GSK, Alka-Seltzer, Wyeth, Roche, Chattem, Amgen

MEDICAL

WHAT YOU NEED TO KNOW

Pharmaceutical companies are some of the most powerful and least responsible of any on the planet. When you do have a choice of medical products, it is very important that you choose the better companies.

BUYING TIPS

✓ Make sure to look on the back of the box to see what company manufactures an item

GREEN HERO

Traditional Medicinals

☆ GAM certified Green Business
☆ Powered by 100% renewable energy
☆ Utilizes sustainable harvesting of wild herbs
☆ Organic, fair trade, biodynamic ingredients

CORPORATE VILLAIN

Pfizer

☠ MM's "Worst Corporation" list for five years[51]
☠ Named "Environmental Laggard" by CEP[14]
☠ #17 in "Top 100 Corporate Criminals"[51]
☠ Paid $171 million to Washington lobbyists[12]
☠ #64 of PERI 100 Most Toxic Water Polluters[58]

MILK & ALTERNATIVES

A	A+	★Organic Valley, Straus Family, Eden Foods, Hemp Bliss, Nancy's
	A	Wildwood, Helios, So Delicious
	A–	Stonyfield Farm, WestSoy
B	B+	Lifeway
	B	Pacific Natural, Clover Stornetta, Zensoy, Smart/Earth Balance
	B–	Vitasoy, Silk
C	C+	
	C	Horizon, *Blue Diamond, Almond Breeze, Hood, Califia*
	C–	8th Continent, Rice/Soy/Almond Dream, Kikkoman
D	D+	Yoo-Hoo
	D	Land O' Lakes
	D–	Alta Dena, Borden, Lactaid, Garelick Farms, Dairy Ease, Meadow Gold, Mayfield, Berkeley Farms
F	F	☠ Knudsen, Nestlé

MILK & ALTERNATIVES

WHAT YOU NEED TO KNOW

Now there is a wide range of socially responsible options for both dairy and non-dairy milk lovers.

GREEN HERO

Organic Valley

☆ Ranked #3 best company on the planet
☆ Small, family farmer-owned co-operative
☆ Humane animal treatment a priority
☆ Gives 10% of profits to local community
☆ Member of the Social Venture Network

CORPORATE VILLAIN

Knudsen (Kraft)

☠ Greenwash Award for public deception[48]
☠ MM's "Worst Corporation" list for five years[51]
☠ Named global climate change laggard[15]
☠ Paid $329 million to Washington lobbyists[12]
☠ Currently the target of 2 major boycotts[22,55]

RESOURCES

💻 www.organicconsumers.org
💻 www.cornucopia.org/dairy_brand_ratings

MOBILE PHONES & SERVICE

A	A+	★Credo Mobile, Working Assets, Better World Telecom
	A	Earth Tones
	A–	Nokia
B	B+	iPhone, Apple, iOS, Google, Android, Pixel
	B	
	B–	Kyocera
C	C+	Vodafone
	C	Motorola, Siemens, Sony *TracFone, Jabra, Cricket*
	C–	HTC, Sanyo, MetroPCS, T-Mobile, LG, Sprint, Virgin, Boost,
D	D+	Samsung, Galaxy
	D	BlackBerry, Acer, Facebook
	D–	Amazon, Fire
F	F	☠ Verizon, Windows Mobile, AT&T, Microsoft

MOBILE PHONES & SERVICE

WHAT YOU NEED TO KNOW

Cell phones are part of a billion-dollar industry. Make sure that this significant revenue stream is going toward building a better world rather than tearing it apart.

BUYING TIPS

✓ Remember to recycle your old cell phone(s)
✓ Look for solar chargers to reduce energy use

GREEN HERO

Credo Mobile (Working Assets)

☆ Given $60 million to a range of nonprofits
☆ Purchases carbon offsets for energy use
☆ Educates for engaged citizenship

CORPORATE VILLAIN

Verizon

☠ Given $245 million to Washington lobbyists[12]
☠ CEP "F" for overall social responsibility[14]
☠ Discriminated against pregnant employees[48]

USEFUL RESOURCES

💻 www.greenpeace.org/greenerelectronics
💻 www.opensecrets.org
💻 www.svtc.org

OFFICE & SCHOOL SUPPLIES

A	**A+**	★Seeds Green Print, Dolphin Blue
	A	ReBinder, The Green Office, GreenerPrinter
	A–	HP, Herman Miller, Xerox
B	**B+**	Ricoh
	B	Staples, DHL, Canon
	B–	Pitney Bowes, IBM
C	**C+**	Hallmark, Crayola, Parker, Shaeffer, Bic
	C	US Post Office, Imation, Ikon, Epson, Brother, *Sanford, Sharpie, Uni-ball, Expo, Zebra, Fiskars, Elmer's, WB Mason, Pentel, Duck, Fellowes, Pilot*
	C–	Airborne Express, Office Depot, OfficeMax, Papermate, Rubbermaid, Henkel
D	**D+**	3M, Scotch, Post-it, Olympus
	D	FedEx, Avery, Smurfit
	D–	UPS, BASF
F	**F**	☠ Mead, Trapper Keeper, At-A-Glance, Day Runner, Cambridge, Columbian, Five Star

OFFICE & SCHOOL SUPPLIES

WHAT YOU NEED TO KNOW

Many of the items we use during the day are in some way related to our workplace. If you have any potential influence over office purchasing, consider suggesting a shift in funds over to more socially responsible products.

GREEN HERO

Seeds Green Printing & Design

☆ GAM & B Lab certified Responsible Business
☆ Environmental leader in the printing industry
☆ 2x named "Best for the World" by B Lab

CORPORATE VILLAIN

Mead (MeadWestvaco)

☠ Named global climate change laggard[19]
☠ Refuses disclosure to consumers[14]
☠ Continues unnecessary animal testing[10]
☠ CEP "F" for overall social responsibility[14]

USEFUL RESOURCES

checkyourpaper.panda.org
www.fsc.org
www.greenamerica.org/livinggreen

OIL, VINEGAR, OLIVES & PICKLES

A	A+	★Canaan Fair Trade, Alter Eco, Dr. Bronner's, Eden, Nutiva
	A	Annie's
	A−	Hain, Spectrum, Hollywood, Napa Valley, Bionaturae, Rapunzel
B	B+	NOW, Bragg, Santa Barbara
	B	Cascadian Farm, Newman's Own, Smart/Earth Balance, Marukan, Natural Value
	B−	Republic of Tea
C	C+	B&G
	C	*Star, Canola Harvest, Saffola, Sagra, Nakano, Lindsay, Vlasic, Armstrong, Mezzetta, Mt. Olive*
	C−	Crisco
D	D+	
	D	Heinz, Mazola, Del Monte
	D−	Wesson, Pam, Bertolli
F	F	☠ Claussen

OIL, VINEGAR, OLIVES & PICKLES

WHAT YOU NEED TO KNOW

A number of socially responsible companies now offer conventional and organic oils and vinegars.

BUYING TIPS

✓ Choose organic oil, vinegar & cooking spray

GREEN HERO

Canaan Fair Trade

☆ GAM certified Green Business
☆ Produces the only fair trade certified olives
☆ Supports Palestinian farmers & communities

CORPORATE VILLAIN

Claussen (Kraft)

☠ Greenwash Award for public deception[48]
☠ MM's "Worst Corporation" list for five years[51]
☠ Named global climate change laggard[15]
☠ Paid $329 million to Washington lobbyists[12]

USEFUL RESOURCES

💻 www.greenpages.org

ONLINE

A	**A+**	
	A	★Etsy, Mozilla, Firefox, Craigslist, Change, Wikipedia, Better World Books, Ethical Ocean, GreenHome
	A–	
B	**B+**	Apple, Safari, Google, Chrome, YouTube
	B	
	B–	SquareSpace, Orbitz
C	**C+**	hulu, eBay, Groupon
	C	Twitter, Expedia, Priceline, Earth-Link, *Snapchat, Instagram, Word-Press, Opera, Netflix*
	C–	LinkedIn, Blizzard, McAfee,
D	**D+**	Cox Cable, DoubleClick, Flickr
	D	Facebook, Charter, yelp, CenturyLink, Qwest, AOL
	D–	Amazon, IMDb, PeopleSoft, Yahoo!, Time Warner
F	**F**	☠ Comcast, Xfinity, Microsoft, Live, Internet Explorer, MSN, Bing, AT&T

ONLINE

WHAT YOU NEED TO KNOW

In the information age, what ISP and browser you use is just as important as where you browse. Whenever possible, support those companies and organizations that turn some of your dollars (and clicks) into making a difference on and offline.

BUYING TIPS

✓ Buy local, used items online when possible
✓ Support open source and community efforts

GREEN HERO

Etsy

☆ B Lab Certified Responsible Company
☆ Major web hub for hand-made goods
☆ Supports thousands of small businesses

CORPORATE VILLAIN

Comcast

☠ CEP & RS "F" for overall social responsibility[61]
☠ Paid $171 million to Washington lobbyists[12]
☠ Gave $38 million in campaign contributions[12]
☠ Refuses disclosure to consumers[14]

OUTDOOR GEAR

A	A+	★Patagonia, ★Klean Kanteen
	A	Teva, Gaiam
	A–	Timberland
B	B+	prAna
	B	REI, Mountain Equipment Co-op
	B–	Kelty, Sierra Designs, LL Bean, Eddie Bauer, Chaco
C	C+	
	C	Marmot, Garmin, Coleman, TomTom, Merrell, Columbia, *Royal Robbins, Nalgene, CamelBak, Keen*
	C–	
D	D+	LuluLemon, Dick's Sporting Goods
	D	
	D–	
F	F	☠Jansport, Eastpak, Eagle Creek, Reef, The North Face

OUTDOOR GEAR

WHAT YOU NEED TO KNOW

While enjoying the outdoors, make certain that the equipment you use is preserving the natural environment rather than helping to destroy it.

GREEN HERO

Patagonia

☆ Environmental leader in industry
☆ Plastic bottles recycling pioneer — fleece
☆ 1% of sales goes to enviro groups
☆ Powered by 100% renewable energy

GREEN HERO

Klean Kanteen

☆ B Lab Certified Responsible Company
☆ GAM certified Green Business
☆ 1% of sales goes to enviro groups

CORPORATE VILLAIN

Jansport (Vanity Fair)

☠ "Bottom Rung," Ladder of Responsibility[40]
☠ Refuses disclosure to consumers[14]
☠ EC responsibility rating of VERY POOR[30]
☠ Named global climate change laggard[19]
☠ CEP "F" for overall social responsibility[14]

PAPER & PAPER PRODUCTS

A	A+	★New Leaf, Seventh Generation, Earth Friendly, Green Forest, Greenline
	A	Living Tree, Sugarmade
	A−	HP, Xerox
B	B+	Mohawk
	B	Cascades, Tork, Staples, Natural Value, Canon
	B−	Scotties, Kleenex, Viva, Scott, Cottonelle, Purely Cotton, IBM
C	C+	Marcal, Earth First
	C	Brother, Epson, *Wausau*, *WB Mason*
	C−	Office Depot, OfficeMax
D	D+	3M, Post-It, Weyerhaeuser
	D	Boise, Domtar, Avery, FedEx
	D−	Hammermill, International Paper
F	F	☠ Georgia-Pacific, Mead, Quilted Northern, Angel Soft, Dixie, Brawny, Sparkle, Mardi Gras, Softly, Bounty, Puffs, Charmin, Ultra, Zee, Envision, Soft n' Gentle, Vanity Fair, Cambridge

PAPER & PAPER PRODUCTS

WHAT YOU NEED TO KNOW

Just remember one thing: PAPER = TREES.

BUYING TIPS

✓ Look for post-consumer recycled content
✓ Choose non-chlorine bleached paper options

GREEN HERO

New Leaf

☆ Forest Stewardship Council certified
☆ Offers 100% post-consumer options
☆ Invented the Eco-Audit for books, etc.
☆ Uses sustainably harvested wood

CORPORATE VILLAIN

Georgia-Pacific (Koch)

☠ #44 in "Top 100 Corporate Criminals"[51]
☠ GP gives lowest environmental ranking[44]
☠ #8 of PERI 100 Most Toxic Air Polluters[58]
☠ Paid $122 million to Washington lobbyists[12]
☠ EC responsibility rating of VERY POOR[30]

USEFUL RESOURCES

💻 checkyourpaper.panda.org
💻 www.fsc.org

PASTA & SAUCE

A	A+	★Eden Foods
	A	★Amy's Kitchen, Simply Organic, Annie's
	A–	Rising Moon, Lundberg, Bionaturae, Garden Time, Walnut Acres, DeBoles
B	B+	Hodgson Mill
	B	Newman's Own, Muir Glen, Natural Value, Betty Crocker
	B–	
C	C+	Seeds of Change
	C	Prego, Campbell's, Progresso, Pasta Roni, Golden Grain, *Barilla, Ronzoni, Stella, Mezzetta, Emeril's, American Beauty, Emilia, Halbrand, De Cecco, Prince, Goya, Manischewitz, DaVinci*
	C–	
D	D+	
	D	Classico, Ragu, McCormick, Lawrys, Contadina, Del Monte, Knorr
	D–	Chef Boyardee, Hunt's, Bertolli
F	F	☠ Back To Nature, Buitoni, Kraft

PASTA & SAUCE

BUYING TIPS

✓ Look for items made with organic ingredients
✓ Buy larger quantities to reduce packaging

GREEN HERO

Eden Foods

☆ Ranked #18 best company on the planet
☆ CEP's highest social responsibility score
☆ GAM certified Green Business

GREEN HERO

Amy's Kitchen

☆ Donates food to relief efforts
☆ Produces all-vegetarian, organic foods
☆ GAM certified Green Business

CORPORATE VILLAIN

Back To Nature (Kraft)

☠ #3 contributor to Washington lobbyists[12]
☠ Currently the target of two major boycotts[22,55]
☠ Greenwash Award for public deception[48]
☠ Part of #2 worst company on the earth[7]

USEFUL RESOURCES

💻 www.greenpages.org
💻 www.organicconsumers.org

PEANUT BUTTER & JELLY

A	A+	
	A	
	A–	★Rapunzel, Crofter's, Bionaturae, Arrowhead Mills, Maranatha
B	B+	Santa Cruz Organic, Woodstock Farms
	B	Smart/Earth Balance, Cascadian Farm
	B–	
C	C+	
	C	Nutella, Seeds of Change, *Joyva, Robertson's, Sorrell Ridge, Glick's, Teddie, Adams, Bonne Maman, Manischewitz*
	C–	Smuckers, Jif, Simply Fruit, Goober, Laura Scudder's, Knott's
D	D+	
	D	Skippy, Welch's
	D–	☠ Peter Pan
F	F	☠ Kraft

PEANUT BUTTER & JELLY

BUYING TIPS

✓ Look for items made with organic ingredients
✓ Seek out local farmers markets

GREEN HERO

Rapunzel

☆ Fair trade & organic leader in food ind.
☆ Supports global sustainable farming
☆ Produced 1st 100% organic chocolate

CORPORATE VILLAIN

Skippy (Unilever)

☠ Continues unnecessary animal testing[10]
☠ EC responsibility rating of VERY POOR[30]
☠ Illegal toxic waste dumping abroad[48]
☠ RS "D-" for overall social responsibility[61]

CORPORATE VILLAIN

Kraft Heinz

☠ Named "Top 10 Greenwasher"[48]
☠ Involved in document deletion cover-up[48]
☠ MM's "Worst Corporation" list for five years[51]
☠ Paid $329 million to Washington lobbyists[12]

PET CARE

A	A+	★BioBag, Only Natural Pet Store
	A	sWheat Scoop, Wildcatch
	A–	Honest Kitchen, Raw Advantage
B	B+	Dr. Harvey's, Natural Balance, V-Dog, Artemis, Halo, PetGuard
	B	Newman's Own, Karma, Heartland, Zuke's, Sensible Choice, AvoDerm, Hill's, Science Diet
	B–	PetCo, Canidae, Happy Dog
C	C+	Castor & Pollux, Wellness
	C	Breeder's Choice, PHD, Old Mother Hubbard, EVO, *Jonny Cat, Nylabone*
	C–	PetSmart
D	D+	
	D	Blue Buffalo, Meow Mix, Milk Bone, 9Lives, Feline Pine, Kibbles 'n Bits, Fresh Step, Scoop Away
	D–	
F	F	☠ Purina, Tidy Cats, Dog Chow, ONE, Advantage/tix, Revolution, Nutro, Frontline, Heartgard, Fancy Feast, Gourmet, IAMS, Sheba, Eukanuba, Tender Vittles, Pedigree, Royal Canin, Alpo, Friskies, Whiskas

PET CARE

WHAT YOU NEED TO KNOW

Recent innovations have been made in the area of socially responsible pet care, so you should have a number of excellent options to choose from.

BUYING TIPS

✓ Buy pet food made with organic ingredients
✓ Buy cat litter made from renewable sources

GREEN HERO

BioBag

☆ 100% biodegradable, corn-based material
☆ 100% compostable w/multiple certifications
☆ GAM certified Green Business

CORPORATE VILLAIN

Purina (Nestlé)

☠ "Most Irresponsible" corporation award[6]
☠ Involved in child slavery lawsuit[61]
☠ Aggressive takeovers of family farms[61]

USEFUL RESOURCES

💻 www.greenpages.org
💻 www.bcorporation.net
💻 www.responsibleshopper.org

POPCORN, NUTS, PRETZELS & MIXES

A	**A+**	★Equal Exchange, ★Eden Foods
	A	
	A–	Arrowhead Mills, Hain, Bearitos, Little Bear
B	**B+**	NOW, Woodstock Farms, Lesser Evil
	B	Newman's Own, Gardetto's, Food Should Taste Good, Chex Mix
	B–	
C	**C+**	
	C	Smartfood, Cracker Jack, Rold Gold, Blue Diamond, *ExpresSnacks, Jolly Time, Yaya's, Sahale, Pretzel Crisps, True North, Pirate's Booty, Snyder's*
	C–	
D	**D+**	
	D	Pop Secret, Emerald
	D–	Act II, Crunch 'n Munch, Jiffy Pop, Orville Redenbacher, Fiddle Faddle, David, Poppycock
F	**F**	☠ Planters, Back to Nature, Corn Nuts

POPCORN, NUTS, PRETZELS & MIXES

WHAT YOU NEED TO KNOW

When you're settling in to watch a little TV or a movie, what you put in that bowl next to the couch makes a big difference for the planet.

GREEN HERO

Equal Exchange

☆ GAM certified Green Business
☆ Business Ethics Award winner
☆ Industry leader in fair trade movement

GREEN HERO

Eden Foods

☆ Ranked #18 best company on the planet
☆ CEP's highest social responsibility score
☆ GAM certified Green Business

CORPORATE VILLAIN

Planters (Kraft)

☠ Part of #2 worst company on the earth[7]
☠ Currently the target of 2 major boycotts[22,55]
☠ #3 contributor to Washington lobbyists[12]

USEFUL RESOURCES

💻 www.responsibleshopper.org

RETAIL STORES

A	**A+**	★Patagonia
	A	
	A–	★Timberland
B	**B+**	Marks & Spencer, Ace Hardware
	B	REI, Nordstrom
	B–	LL Bean, Eddie Bauer, IKEA
C	**C+**	
	C	Best Buy, *Neiman Marcus*
	C–	Talbot's
D	**D+**	Dollar General, Dick's Sporting Goods, Land's End
	D	Bed Bath & Beyond, Long's Drugs, Rite Aid, BJ's, Saks Fifth Avenue, JC Penney, Ross, Kohl's
	D–	Hudson's, Marshall Field, Big Lots, Target, Dillards, Walgreens, Home Depot, Lowe's, Marshall's, TJ Maxx
F	**F**	☠ Walmart, Sam's Club, CVS, Sears, Kmart, Orchard Supply Hardware, Bloomingdale's, Macy's, Foley's, North Face

RETAIL STORES

GREEN HERO

Patagonia

☆ Environmental leader in industry
☆ Plastic bottles recycling pioneer — fleece
☆ 1% of sales goes to enviro groups
☆ Powered by 100% renewable energy

GREEN HERO

Timberland

☆ Business Ethics Award winner
☆ 4x Named World's Most Ethical Company
☆ Labelling leader, eco-social footprint
☆ EPA Green Power Award winner

CORPORATE VILLAIN

Walmart

☠ #3 worst company on the planet[7]
☠ CEP "F" for overall social responsibility[14]
☠ Sex-discrimination class-action lawsuit[48]
☠ Documented exploitation of child labor[61]
☠ Paid $75 million to Washington lobbyists[12]
☠ RS rated worst responsibility in industry[61]

USEFUL RESOURCES

💻 www.opensecrets.org
💻 www.responsibleshopper.org

RICE & OTHER GRAINS

A	A+	★Alter Eco, Eden, Lotus Foods, ★Canaan Fair Trade
	A	Fantastic Foods
	A–	Lundberg, Casbah
B	B+	
	B	Annie Chun's, Betty Crocker
	B–	
C	C+	
	C	Seeds Of Change, Near East, Rice-A-Roni, Quaker *Minute Rice, Dynasty, Carolina, Mrs. Cubbison's, Mahatma, Success Rice, Goya, Manischewitz*
	C–	Hungry Jack
D	D+	Lipton
	D	McCormick, S&W, Hormel
	D–	
F	F	☠ Uncle Ben's, Kraft, Knorr

RICE & OTHER GRAINS

BUYING TIPS

✓ Look for organic grains
✓ Buy in bulk to reduce packaging waste

GREEN HERO

Alter Eco

☆ Produces a range of 100% fair trade goods
☆ Works directly with local farmer cooperatives
☆ GAM certified Green Business
☆ Fair trade consumer education leader

GREEN HERO

Canaan Fair Trade

☆ GAM certified Green Business
☆ Leader in fair trade integrity standards
☆ Supports Palestinian farmers & communities

CORPORATE VILLAIN

Uncle Ben's (Mars)

☠ CEP "F" for overall social responsibility[14]
☠ On MM's "10 Worst Corporations" list[51]
☠ Evidence of involvement in child slave labor[61]
☠ Target of international fair trade campaign[25]
☠ "Bottom Rung," Ladder of Responsibility[40]

SALSA, SPREADS & DIPS

A	A+	
	A	★Emerald Valley, Fantastic Foods, ★Amy's, Simply Organic, Wildwood
	A–	Walnut Acres, Bearitos, Casbah, Rising Moon
B	B+	
	B	Muir Glen, Newman's Own
	B–	Pace, Laura Scudder's
C	C+	
	C	Seeds Of Change, Old El Paso, Lay's, Fritos, Sabra, Tostitos, *Nonna Lena's, Salpica, Frontera, Raquel's, Gringo, Micaelas, Green Mountain, Cedar's, Litehouse, Haig's, Ortega, Native, Margaritaville, Mrs. Renfros*
	C–	
D	D+	Lipton
	D	La Victoria, Chi Chi's
	D–	Rosarita
F	F	☠ Taco Bell, Kraft

SALSA, SPREADS & DIPS

WHAT YOU NEED TO KNOW

This category includes everything from hummus to salsa to bean dip, and there are responsible choices to be had for every one.

GREEN HERO

Emerald Valley

☆ Socially Responsible Business Award
☆ 1% to humanitarian & ecological causes
☆ Green Business of the Year Award

GREEN HERO

Amy's Kitchen

☆ Donates food to relief efforts
☆ Produces all-vegetarian, organic foods
☆ GAM certified Green Business

CORPORATE VILLAIN

Taco Bell (Kraft)

☠ Named "Top 10 Greenwasher"[48]
☠ Involved in document deletion cover-up[48]
☠ MM's "Worst Corporation" list for five years[51]
☠ Paid $329 million to Washington lobbyists[12]

SEAFOOD I

A	A+	★Henry & Lisa's
	A	★Wildcatch, Wild Planet, Pelican's Choice, Wild Pacific, Vital Choice
	A–	Blue Horizon Organic, RainCoast
B	B+	Whole Foods*
	B	Safeway*, Von's*, Pak N Save*, Wegmans*, HyVee*
	B–	Trader Joe's*, Ahold*, Giant*, Aldi*, Stop & Shop*, Target*
C	C+	Delhaize*, Fry's*, Food Lion*
	C	Shop N Save*, Costco*, Sam's Club*, Raleys*, Asda*, C&S*, Fresh & Easy*, Albertson's*, Walmart*
	C–	Hannaford*, Shop Rite*, Meijer*, Giant Eagle*, Harris Teeter*
D	D+	Price Chopper*, H E Butt*, Kroger*, Food 4 Less*, Quik Stop*, King Soopers*, Ralph's*, Wakefern*
	D	WinCo*, Cub Foods*, Shaw's*, Lucky*, Sav A Lot*, Star*, Biggs*
	D–	Roundy's*, Bumble Bee
F	F	☠ Winn-Dixie*, Save Mart*, Publix*, Bi-Lo*, A&P*

SEAFOOD I

WHAT YOU NEED TO KNOW

One of the most important changes you can make is in choosing ecologically responsible seafood. While seafood brands are rated in the usual way in the chart on the left, supermarkets are also rated here solely based on the sustainability of their seafood selection and are noted with an asterisk (*).

BUYING TIPS

✓ Look for sustainable fishing labels
✓ Local freshwater is often a good choice
✓ See next section for more seafood guidance

GREEN HERO

Henry & Lisa's

☆ Only environmentally sustainable fishing
☆ Conservation scientists advisory board
☆ Result of marine conservation groups

GREEN HERO

Wildcatch

☆ Certified by Marine Stewardship Council
☆ Harvests only sustainable, wild seafood
☆ Works with nonprofits like Salmon Nation

USEFUL RESOURCES

💻 cato.greenpeaceusa.org

SEAFOOD II

A	**A**	Arctic Char, Mackerel, Mussels, Salmon (Wild Alaskan), Striped Bass
B	**B**	Abalone, Barramundi, Black Cod, Catfish, Oysters, Perch, Prawn, Sablefish, Sardines, Scallops, Snow Crab, Sole, Squid, Tilapia, Trout
C	**C**	Clams, Cod, Crawfish, Dogfish, Dungeness Crab, Flounder, Haddock, Halibut, Herring, Mahimahi, Monkfish, Pollock, Rockfish, Salmon (all other), Shrimp, Smelt, Snapper, Wahoo, Walleye, Whitefish, Yellowtail
D	**D**	Anchovies, Blue Crab, Grouper, Lobster, Ray, Sea Bass, Skate, Swordfish, Tuna
F	**F**	Caviar, Eel, King Crab, Marlin, Octopus, Orange Roughy, Oreos, Shark, Sturgeon

SEAFOOD II

WHAT YOU NEED TO KNOW

Our current fishing practices are destroying ocean life at an unprecedented rate. Rather than ranking companies, the chart to the left shows which species are being more sustainably harvested and which are being fished out of existence based on a synthesis of available data from the four major organizations researching this issue: *Marine Conservation Society, Monterey Bay Aquarium, Environmental Defense Fund* and *The Safina Center* (formerly *Blue Ocean Institute*). It also takes into account the environmental costs of harvesting each kind of seafood. Use it both at the supermarket seafood counter and when you go out to eat.

BUYING TIPS

✓ When it's unclear, ask the deli staffer or server for more specifics about the fish

✓ When category A or B seafood is not available, consider non-seafood alternatives

USEFUL RESOURCES

- www.fishonline.org
- www.seafoodwatch.org
- seafood.edf.org
- www.safinacenter.org

SHOES

A	A+	★Dansko, Patagonia
	A	Simple Shoes, Sole Rebels, Therafit, Newton Running
	A–	Birkenstock, Timberland
B	B+	
	B	Teva, UGG, Sanuk, Zappos, Red Wing
	B–	Chaco
C	C+	Nike, Reebok, Adidas, DMX, Puma, New Balance, Rockport, Nunn Bush
	C	Ecco, Salomon, Dunlop, Everlast, Hush Puppies, Umbro, Ellesse, HI-TEC, Merrell, *Crocs, Keen, DC*
	C–	FILA, K-Swiss, Brooks, Lotto
D	D+	Stride Rite, Keds, Sperry, Pentland, Tommy Hilfiger
	D	Converse, Florsheim, Saucony
	D–	Foot Locker, ASICS, Mizuno
F	F	☠ LA Gear, Vans, Reef, Skechers, DISCOUNT & DEPARTMENT STORE BRANDS

SHOES

WHAT YOU NEED TO KNOW

Almost all store-bought shoes are made in factories in the developing world. The real questions are, How are the workers treated? Are they safe? And do they make enough of a wage to live decently? Your choices here will determine the answers to those questions for tens of thousands of families.

GREEN HERO

Dansko

☆ GAM certified Green Business
☆ Powered by 100% renewable energy
☆ LEED Gold eco-certified main office

CORPORATE VILLAIN

LA Gear

☠ Named "Sweatshop Laggard"[14]
☠ CEP "F" for overall social responsibility[14]
☠ Weak supplier code of conduct for workers[14]

USEFUL RESOURCES

- www.cleanclothes.org
- en.maquilasolidarity.org
- www.free2work.org
- www.labourbehindthelabel.org

SOAP

A	A+	★Dr. Bronner's, Canaan Fair Trade, ★Pangea Organics, EO, Method, Aubrey Organics
	A	Juniper Ridge, Kiss My Face, Auromere, Oregon Soap Co.
	A–	Jäsön, Tom's of Maine, Tender Care, Alba
B	B+	
	B	Body Shop, Sappo Hill, Irish Spring, Softsoap, Palmolive, Zum Bar, Hugo
	B–	Shikai, Clearly Natural
C	C+	Burt's Bees, Nature's Gate
	C	Avalon Organics, *Plantlife, Germ-X*
	C–	Nivea, Coastal
D	D+	
	D	St. Ives, Dove, Lever 2000, Caress, Axe, Suave
	D–	Dial, Tone, Pure & Natural, Coast, Aveeno, Purell
F	F	☠ Ivory, Safeguard, Olay, Zest, Gillette, Old Spice, Lava

SOAP

BUYING TIPS

✓ Choose soaps that aren't tested on animals
✓ Buy USDA Certified BioBased soaps

GREEN HERO

Dr. Bronner's

☆ Leader in organic standards integrity
☆ 5:1 CEO to worker salary cap
☆ Profits donated to variety of causes
☆ Liquid soaps in 100% recycled plastic
☆ Does not test on animals

GREEN HERO

Pangea Organics

☆ GAM certified Green Business
☆ Never tests on ingredients on animals
☆ 2x Award Winner for Business Ethics

CORPORATE VILLAIN

Ivory (Procter & Gamble)

☠ MM's "Worst Corporation" list for two years[51]
☠ Continues unnecessary animal testing[10]
☠ "Bottom Rung," Ladder of Responsibility[40]
☠ Spent over $68 million on lobbyists[12]

SODA

A	A+	
	A	★Maine Root
	A–	Chill, Oogave, Sipp
B	B+	Blue Sky, Santa Cruz Organic, Steaz, Hansen's
	B	Newman's Own, Izze
	B–	
C	C+	
	C	Tropicana, Mug, Pepsi, Mountain Dew, Sierra Mist, Slice, *Bawls, Moxie, Reed's, Shasta, Jolt*
	C–	R.W. Knudsen, Polar, Jones, Thomas Kemper, Weight Watchers, Arizona, Soda Stream, Crystal Geyser, Boylan
D	D+	Orangina, 7-Up, Snapple, A&W, Diet Rite, Squirt, Sunkist, Welch's, IBC, Stewart's, Dr. Pepper, Canada Dry, Crush, RC Cola, Hires, Lipton
	D	Henry Weinhard's
	D–	
F	F	☠ Coca-Cola, Sprite, Fanta, Pibb Xtra, Barq's, Minute Maid, San Pellegrino, Fresca, Tab

SODA

WHAT YOU NEED TO KNOW

If you're like most people, soda is a daily part of your diet. Move up on the responsible soda chain to avoid companies that are wrecking the planet.

BUYING TIPS

✓ Buy soda in aluminum or glass containers

GREEN HERO

Maine Root

☆ Offers fair trade certified sodas
☆ Organic soda industry leader
☆ Local deliveries made using biodiesel
☆ Supports sustainable farming practices

CORPORATE VILLAIN

Coca-Cola

☠ MM's "Worst Corporation" list for three years[51]
☠ Hinders clean water access abroad[22]
☠ Target of major human rights boycotts[30]

USEFUL RESOURCES

- www.ethicalconsumer.org
- www.multinationalmonitor.org
- www.stopcorporateabuse.org

SOUPS, NOODLES & CURRIES

A	**A+**	★Eden Foods
	A	Amy's, Annie's, Fantastic Foods
	A–	Native Forest, Organic Planet, Nile Spice, Health Valley, Walnut Acres, Edward & Sons, Rapunzel, Imagine, Casbah
B	**B+**	Pacific Natural, Nasoya
	B	Muir Glen, Progresso
	B–	
C	**C+**	
	C	Campbell's, Wolfgang Puck, Seeds of Change, *Annie Chun's, Spice Hunter, Dr. McDougall's, Swanson, Maruchan, Nissin, Tasty Bite, Sun Luck, Alessi, Snow's, Bar Harbor, Bear Creek*
	C–	Thai Kitchen
D	**D+**	Lipton, Cup-A-Soup
	D	Knorr, Mrs. Grass, Herb Ox
	D–	☠ Healthy Choice
F	**F**	

SOUPS, NOODLES & CURRIES

WHAT YOU NEED TO KNOW

Whether it's instant noodles or pea soup, there are many excellent choices for hot, steaming, socially responsible meals.

BUYING TIPS

✓ Look for soups made with organic ingredients

GREEN HERO

Eden Foods

☆ Ranked #18 best company on the planet
☆ CEP's highest social responsibility score
☆ GAM certified Green Business

CORPORATE VILLAIN

Healthy Choice (ConAgra)

☠ MM's "Worst Corporation" list for two years[51]
☠ #50 in "Top 100 Corporate Criminals"[51]
☠ Ceres "Climate Change Laggard"[15]

USEFUL RESOURCES

- www.responsibleshopper.org
- www.multinationalmonitor.org
- www.ceres.org

SUGAR, SPICES & SWEETENERS

A	A+	★Wholesome Sweeteners, Eden, Alter Eco, King Arthur, Canaan Fair Trade, Equal Exchange, Frontier, Simply Organic
	A	
	A−	Lundberg, Hain, Spicely, Silk Road, Coombs, Great Northern
B	B+	NOW, Florida Crystals, Bragg
	B	
	B−	
C	C+	
	C	Mrs. Butterworth's, *Domino, Sweet 'N Low, Butter Buds, C&H, Spice Hunter, Goya, Morton, Sugar in the Raw, Spike*
	C−	Spice Islands
D	D+	
	D	McCormick, Lawry's, Schilling, Mrs. Dash, Hormel, Sugar Twin, Adolph's, Molly McButter
	D−	Splenda
F	F	☠ Nutrasweet, Equal, Monsanto

SUGAR, SPICES & SWEETENERS

WHAT YOU NEED TO KNOW

Many of these items we buy once and keep using for years. If you want to make a difference while saving your budget, start here.

BUYING TIPS

✓ Buy in bulk to reduce packaging waste

GREEN HERO

Wholesome Sweeteners

☆ 1st US fair trade certified sugar available
☆ Actively supports sustainable farming
☆ Makes a full line of organic sweeteners

CORPORATE VILLAIN

Nutrasweet (Monsanto)

☠ MM's "Worst Corporation" list for three years[51]
☠ #72 of PERI 100 Most Toxic Air Polluters[58]
☠ Paid $80 million to Washington lobbyists[12]
☠ RS "D-" for overall social responsibility[61]

USEFUL RESOURCES

💻 www.free2work.org
💻 www.organicconsumers.org
💻 www.responsibleshopper.org

SUPERMARKETS

A	A+	FOOD CO-OPS, FARMERS MARKETS
	A	
	A−	★Whole Foods
B	B+	
	B	Trader Joe's, Wegmans, Raley's,
	B−	Sainsbury's, HyVee
C	C+	Fresh & Easy, Food Lion
	C	Delhaize, Asda, Wakefern, Nugget, Pathmark, No Frills, Smith's, Fry's
	C−	Sprouts, Price Chopper, WinCo, Giant Eagle, C&S, Harris Teeter
D	D+	Hannaford, Shop 'n Save, Shop Rite, H.E.B
	D	Von's, Pak 'n Save, Safeway, Aldi, Stop & Shop, Giant, Peapod, Rite Aid, BJ's, Save Mart, Meijer, A&P, Star, Roundy's, Albertson's, Cub, Lucky's, Save-A-Lot, Shaw's, Publix, Long's
	D−	Target, BiLo, WinnDixie, Walgreens
F	F	☠ Walmart, CVS, Ralph's, Food 4 Less, Fred Meyer, King Soopers, QFC, Kroger, Kwik Shop, Quick Stop, Loaf 'N Jug, Costco

SUPERMARKETS

WHAT YOU NEED TO KNOW

If you have a choice, changing where you shop is an incredibly powerful action that will support people and the planet above profit.

GREEN HERO

Whole Foods

☆ BE's "Best Corporations" list for three years
☆ HQ Powered by 100% renewable energy
☆ Business Ethics Award winner
☆ Established animal & poverty foundation
☆ Created animal compassion standards
☆ Leader in sourcing sustainable seafood

CORPORATE VILLAIN

Walmart

☠ MM's "Worst Corporation" list for three years[51]
☠ Major toxic-waste-dumping fines[25]
☠ #3 worst company on the planet[4]
☠ CEP "F" for overall social responsibility[14]
☠ Documented exploitation of child labor[61]
☠ Paid $75 million to Washington lobbyists[12]

USEFUL RESOURCES

💻 www.localharvest.org
💻 www.cooperativegrocer.coop

TEA

A	A+	★Numi, Traditional Medicinals, ★Equal Exchange, Choice, Eco Teas, Guayaki, Tulsi, Organic India
	A	Zhena's Gypsy, Rishi, Sencha, Oregon Chai, Bhakti, Davidson's Organics, Arbor Teas
	A−	Kopali, Honest Tea, Bionaturae, Celestial Seasonings
B	B+	Mighty Leaf, Tao of Tea, Pacific Natural
	B	Newman's Own
	B−	Tazo, Republic Of Tea, Bigelow
C	C+	Stash
	C	*Ito En, Yogi, Harney & Sons, Triple Leaf, Coffee Bean & Tea Leaf*
	C−	Arizona, Twinings, Jones, Tejava
D	D+	Lipton, Good Earth, Tetley, Snapple
	D	Red Rose
	D−	
F	F	☠ Nestlé, PG Tips, Sweet Leaf, Nestlé

TEA

WHAT YOU NEED TO KNOW

If you drink tea, you have an incredible selection of human and planet-friendly varieties to pick from.

BUYING TIPS

✓ Look first for the fair trade label, then move on to organic, sustainably harvested, etc.

GREEN HERO

Numi

☆ GAM certified Green Business
☆ Member of the Social Venture Network
☆ Socially Responsible Business Award

GREEN HERO

Equal Exchange

☆ GAM certified Green Business
☆ Business Ethics Award winner
☆ Industry leader in fair trade movement

CORPORATE VILLAIN

Nestea (Nestlé)

☠ Involved in child slavery lawsuit[61]
☠ Baby formula human rights boycott[48]
☠ Involved in union busting outside US[61]
☠ "Most Irresponsible" corporation award[6]

TOYS & GAMES

A	A+	
	A	★Hazelnut Kids, Naturally Playful, Reach & Teach
	A–	Down to Earth Toys, Eco Toy Town
B	B+	Mac, iOS, Android
	B	Hot Wheels, Mattel, Matchbox
	B–	Lego
C	C+	Electronic Arts, Crayola
	C	Sony, Playstation, *Wham-O, Sega, Namco, Ubisoft, Square Enix*
	C–	Blizzard, Activision, Fisher Price, GameStop
D	D+	Toys R Us, Babies R Us, Kids R Us
	D	Playskool, Hasbro, Parker Brothers, Wizards of the Coast, Play-Doh, Nerf, Milton Bradley, Transformers, Tonka
	D–	Nintendo, Wii, Disney, Warner Bros.
F	F	☠ Xbox, Microsoft, Window, PC

TOYS & GAMES

WHAT YOU NEED TO KNOW

The irresponsible manufacturing of toys and games does not always directly threaten us or our children, but it always endangers people or the environment in some part of the world.

BUYING TIPS

✓ Look for less common, cooperative games
✓ Buy used toys and games when available
✓ Seek out shareware and open source games

GREEN HERO

Hazlenut Kids

☆ GAM certified Green Business
☆ Online hub for sustainable and ethical toys
☆ 2x named Green Business of the Year

CORPORATE VILLAIN

Xbox (Microsoft)

☠ Named "abusive monopoly" by US Court[48]
☠ Paid $150 million to Washington lobbyists[12]
☠ Greenpeace "Green Electronics Laggard"[44]
☠ Refuses disclosure on its business[14]

USEFUL RESOURCES

💻 www.greenpeace.org
💻 www.free2work.org

TRAVEL

A	**A+**	★TerraPass, Patagonia
	A	Native Energy, Carbonfund, ZipCar, CouchSurfing Intl.
	A–	Timberland
B	**B+**	Google Flights
	B	
	B–	Orbitz, CarbonNeutral, Kelty
C	**C+**	Holland America Cruises, High Sierra, Samsonite
	C	Amtrak, Expedia, Hotels.com, Hertz, Thrifty, Dollar, Carnival Cruises, *Priceline, TripAdvisor, Kayak*
	C–	Enterprise, Avis, Princess Cruises, Regency Cruises
D	**D+**	
	D	Yelp, Royal Caribbean Cruises
	D–	
F	**F**	☠Jansport, Eagle Creek, North Face

TRAVEL

WHAT YOU NEED TO KNOW

While categories like airlines and hotels are large enough to be listed separately, this chart includes everything else you might need on your travels: luggage, car rentals, cruise lines, travel sites and carbon offset services.

GREEN HERO

TerraPass

☆ B Lab Certified Responsible Company
☆ GAM certified Green Business
☆ Achieved Greenopia's highest eco-score

CORPORATE VILLAIN

Jansport (Vanity Fair)

☠ "Bottom Rung," Ladder of Responsibility[40]
☠ Refuses disclosure to consumers[14]
☠ EC responsibility rating of VERY POOR[30]
☠ Named global climate change laggard[19]
☠ CEP "F" for overall social responsibility[14]

USEFUL RESOURCES

💻 sustainabletravelinternational.org
💻 www.gstcouncil.org

VITAMINS

A	**A+**	
	A	★New Chapter, I Am Enlightened, Deva, The Honest Company, Garden of Life
	A−	Oregon's Wild Harvest
B	**B+**	NOW, Rainbow Light
	B	Nature's Way
	B−	Solgar, Nutribiotic
C	**C+**	Nature's Own, Sundown Naturals, Viactiv
	C	GNC, *Earthrise, Nature's Life, All One, Solaray, VegiLife, Nature Made, Natrol, SuperNutrition, Emergen-C, Jarrow, Carlson, Twinlab, Nature's Plus, Nature's Bounty, Weil, Source Naturals, Country Life, Wellesse*
	C−	
D	**D+**	
	D	
	D−	
F	**F**	☠ Centrum, Pfizer, Flintstones, ☠ One-A-Day, Bayer, Wyeth, Similac

VITAMINS

BUYING TIPS

✓ Look for organic ingredients in supplements
✓ Buy in recyclable bottles: #1, #2, or glass
✓ Purchase in bulk to reduce packaging waste

GREEN HERO

New Chapter

☆ Organic, sustainable, harvesting practices
☆ International biodynamic certification
☆ Extensive environmental awards
☆ Promotes efforts to sustain biodiversity

CORPORATE VILLAIN

One-A-Day (Bayer)

☠ #3 of PERI 100 Most Toxic Air Polluters[58]
☠ #78 of PERI 100 Most Toxic Water Polluters[58]
☠ Paid $70 million to Washington lobbyists[12]
☠ MM's "Worst Corporation" list for two years[51]
☠ BD's "Most Irresponsible" corporation award[6]

CORPORATE VILLAIN

Centrum (Pfizer)

☠ #64 of PERI 100 Most Toxic Water Polluters[58]
☠ #17 in "Top 100 Corporate Criminals"[51]
☠ Paid $171 million to Washington lobbyists[12]
☠ MM's "Worst Corporation" list for four years[51]

WATER

A	A+	★Klean Kanteen, TAP / FILTERED
	A	
	A-	Earth Water
B	B+	
	B	Evian, Volvic, Dannon
	B-	Saratoga
C	C+	Fiji
	C	Voss, Propel, Aquafina, SoBe, *La Croix, Hawaii, Icelandic Glacial, Penta, Essentia, Crystal Springs, Sparkletts, Trinity, Adirondack, Ice Age*
	C-	Ethos, Crystal Geyser, Arizona, Fruit2O, Metro Mint
D	D+	Deja Blue, Schweppes, Snapple
	D	K2O
	D-	
F	F	☠ Dasani, Glaceau, Vitamin Water, ☠ Arrowhead, Vittel, Perrier, Poland Spring, Deer Park, Calistoga, Smart Water, S. Pellegrino, Zephyr Hills, Ozarka, Ice Mountain, Acqua Panna

WATER

BUYING TIPS

✓ Carry your own reusable bottle
✓ Buy fewer, larger bottles, and refill them
✓ ALWAYS recycle the bottles when done

GREEN HERO

Klean Kanteen

☆ B Lab Certified Responsible Company
☆ GAM certified Green Business
☆ 1% of sales goes to enviro groups

CORPORATE VILLAIN

Arrowhead (Nestlé)

☠ Baby formula human rights boycott[48]
☠ "Most Irresponsible" corporation award[6]
☠ Involved in child slavery lawsuit[61]

CORPORATE VILLAIN

Dasani (Coca Cola)

☠ MM's "Worst Corporation" list for three years[51]
☠ Hinders clean water access abroad[22]
☠ Target of major human rights boycotts[30]

USEFUL RESOURCES

www.thinkoutsidethebottle.org
www.greenpeace.org

WINE

A	A+	LOCAL VINEYARDS, ★Frey
	A	★Fetzer, La Rocca, Frog's Leap,
	A–	Kunde Estate, Alma Rosa
B	B+	Banrock Station, Rodney Strong, Sobon Estate, St Francis, Bota Box
	B	Lemelson, Mountain Meadows, Cline, Kendall Jackson
	B–	French Rabbit, Benziger
C	C+	Sutter Home, Turning Leaf, Grgich Hills, Ecco Domani, Luna di Luna
	C	Lindemans, Almaden, Jacob's Creek, Glen Ellen, Columbia Crest, Bogle, Inglenook, Delicato, Woodbridge, Franzia, Paul Masson, Estancia
	C–	Dom Perignon, Krug, Bonny Doon, Beringer, Mondavi, Sterling, Cloudy Bay, Blossom Hill, Corbett Canyon
D	D+	Charles Shaw, Barefoot, Yellow Tail, Gallo, Korbel, Carlo Rossi, Andre
	D	
	D–	
F	F	☠ Chateau Ste Michelle

WINE

BUYING TIPS

✓ Look for organic wine varieties on the shelf
✓ Support local vineyards — try their wine
✓ Buy in bulk to reduce packaging waste

GREEN HERO

Fetzer

☆ Powered by 100% renewable energy
☆ All vineyards certified organic
☆ Reduced production waste by 94%
☆ Bottles are 40% recycled glass
☆ BE Award for Environmental Excellence

GREEN HERO

Frey

☆ GAM certified Green Business
☆ Oldest organic US winery
☆ 1st US biodynamic wine producer

CORPORATE VILLAIN

Chateau Ste Michelle (Altria)

☠ Named "Top 10 Greenwasher"[48]
☠ Involved in document deletion cover-up[48]
☠ MM's "Worst Corporation" list for five years[51]
☠ Paid $329 million to Washington lobbyists[12]

PRODUCT CATEGORY INDEX

CAN'T FIND...	LOOK UNDER...
Antiperspirant	Body Care
Apple Sauce	Canned Goods
Bandages	Medical
Barbeque Sauce	Condiments & Dressings
Batteries	Electronics
Beans	Canned Goods
Bottled Water	Water & Water Bottles
Bouillon	Soup, Noodles & Curries
Car Rental	Travel
Carbon Offsets	Travel
Cell Phones	Mobile Phones & Service
Chicken	Meat Products
Cocoa	Chocolate
Cold Remedies	Medical
Corn Meal	Baked Goods & Baking Supplies
Couscous	Rice & Other Grains
Cottage Cheese	Dairy Products
Cough Drops	Medical
Crackers	Cookies & Crackers
Cream Cheese	Dairy Products

Creamer	Coffee
Credit Cards	Banks & Credit Cards
Croutons	Condiments & Dressings
Cruise Lines	Travel
Curries	Soup, Noodles & Curries
Deodorant	Body Care
Department Stores	Retail Stores
Detergents	Laundry Supplies
Diapers	Baby Care
Dips	Salsa, Spreads & Dips
Dishwashing Liquid	Cleaning Products
Evaporated Milk	Baked Goods & Baking Supplies
Fish	Seafood
Flour	Baked Goods & Baking Supplies
French Fries	Fruits & Vegetables
Games	Toys & Games
Granola Bars	Energy Bars
Grocery Stores	Supermarkets
Hardware	Appliances & Hardware
Honey	Sugar, Spices & Sweeteners
Hummus	Salsa, Spreads & Dips
Jams & Jellies	Peanut Butter & Jelly
Ketchup	Condiments & Dressings
Lip Balm	Body Care
Luggage	Travel

Margarine	Butter & Margarine
Marshmallows	Baked Goods & Baking Supplies
Mayonnaise	Condiments & Dressings
Mouthwash	Dental Care
Mustard	Condiments & Dressings
Noodles	Soup, Noodles & Curries
Nuts	Popcorn, Nuts, Pretzels & Mixes
Package Delivery	Office & School Supplies
Pain Relievers	Medical
Pancake Mix	Breakfast Food
Pencils & Pens	Office & School Supplies
Pickles	Oil, Vinegar, Olives & Pickles
Pies	Desserts
Pizza	Frozen Dinners
Potato Chips	Chips
Pretzels	Popcorn, Nuts, Pretzels & Mixes
Pudding	Dairy Products
Relishes	Oil, Vinegar, Olives & Pickles
Rice Milk	Milk & Alternatives
Salt	Sugar, Spices & Sweeteners

School Supplies	Office & School Supplies
Shampoo	Hair Care
Shaving Needs	Body Care
Soft Drinks	Soda
Soy Milk	Milk & Alternatives
Sports Drinks	Energy Drinks
Stuffing Mix	Bread
Sun Block	Body Care
Syrup	Sugar, Spices & Sweeteners
Tahini	Peanut Butter & Jelly
Tampons	Feminine Care
Tape	Office & School Supplies
Tissues	Paper & Paper Products
Tofu	Meat Alternatives
Toilet Paper	Paper & Paper Products
Tomato Paste	Pasta & Sauce
Toothbrushes	Dental Care
Toothpaste	Dental Care
Tuna	Seafood
Veggie Burgers	Meat Alternatives
Vinegar	Oil, Vinegar, Olives & Pickles
Video Games	Toys & Games
Waffles	Breakfast Food
Whipped Cream	Dairy Products
Yogurt	Dairy Products

DATA SOURCES

1. 1% For The Planet [onepercentfortheplanet.org]
2. American Humane [americanhumane.org]
3. American Sustainable Business Council [asbcouncil.org]
4. As You Sow [asyousow.org]
5. B Corporations [bcorporation.net]
6. Berne Declaration [bernedeclaration.ch]
7. Better World Shopper [betterworldshopper.org]
8. Business Ethics [business-ethics.com]
9. Business for Social Responsibility [bsr.org]
10. Caring Consumer [caringconsumer.org]
11. Center for Public Integrity [publicintegrity.org]
12. Center For Responsive Politics [opensecrets.org]
13. Center For Science In The Public Interest [cspinet.org]
14. CEP (Council on Economic Priorities) [archive.org]
15. CERES [ceres.org]
16. Clean Clothes Campaign [cleanclothes.org]
17. Clean Computer Campaign [svtc.org]
18. Clean Up Fashion [labourbehindthelabel.org]
19. Climate Counts [climatecounts.org]
20. Consumers Union [consumersunion.org]
21. Cornucopia Institute [cornucopia.org]
22. Corporate Accountability International [stopcorporateabuse.org]
23. Corporate Critic [corporatecritic.org]
24. Corporate Knights [corporateknights.com]
25. Corpwatch [corpwatch.org]

DATA SOURCES

26. Covalence EthicalQuote [covalence.ch]
27. CSRwire [csrwire.com]
28. Electronic Industry Citizenship Coalition [eiccoalition.org]
29. Electronics TakeBack Coalition [electronicstakeback.com]
30. Ethical Consumer [ethicalconsumer.org]
31. Ethical Trading Initiative [ethicaltrade.org]
32. Ethisphere [ethisphere.com]
33. Fair Labor Association [fairlabor.org]
34. Fair Trade Federation [fairtradefederation.org]
35. Fast Company [fastcompany.com]
36. Forest Ethics [forestethics.org]
37. Free2Work [free2work.org]
38. Global Exchange [globalexchange.org]
39. Global Sullivan Principles [thesullivanfoundation.org/gsp]
40. Green America [greenamerica.org]
41. Green Cross International [gci.ch]
42. Green-e [green-e.org]
43. Greenopia [greenopia.com]
44. Greenpeace [greenpeace.org]
45. Hoovers [hoovers.com]
46. Human Rights Campaign [hrc.org]
47. International Labor Rights Forum [laborrights.org]
48. Know More [archive.org]

DATA SOURCES

49. Labour Behind The Label
[labourbehindthelabel.org]
50. Maquila Solidarity Network [maquilasolidarity.org]
51. Multinational Monitor [multinationalmonitor.org]
52. National Association for the Advancement of Colored People [naacp.org]
53. Natural Resources Defense Council [nrdc.org]
54. *The New York Times* [newyorktimes.com]
55. Organic Consumers Assn [organicconsumers.org]
56. Oxfam International [oxfam.org]
57. Oceana International [oceana.org]
58. Political Economy Research Institute [peri.umass.edu]
59. Rainforest Action Network [ran.org]
60. Responsible Purchasing Network [responsiblepurchasing.org]
61. Responsible Shopper [responsibleshopper.org]
62. Responsible Sourcing Network [sourcingnetwork.org]
63. Restaurant Opportunities Centers United [rocunited.org]
64. Sierra Club [sierraclub.org]
65. Social Accountability International [sai-intl.org]
66. Social Venture Network [svn.org]
67. Socially Responsible Business Awards [sociallyresponsibleawards.org]
68. Transfair USA [transfairusa.org]
69. Union of Concerned Scientists [ucsusa.org]

DATA SOURCES

70. U.S. Environmental Protection Agency [epa.gov]
71. U.S. Securities & Exchange Commission [sec.gov]
72. Vegan Action [vegan.org]
73. *The Washington Post* [washingtonpost.com]
74. WorldBlu [worldblu.com]
75. World Environment Center [wec.org]
76. World Wildlife Fund [worldwildlife.org]

About the Author

Since receiving his doctoral degree in sociology from the University of Colorado, Boulder, Ellis Jones has focused all of his energies on bridging the gap between academics, activists, and the average citizen. A scholar of social responsibility, global citizenship, and everyday activism, Dr. Jones continues to teach and give presentations across the country on how to turn lofty ideals into practical actions. His other work includes *The Better World Handbook* (winner of *Spirituality & Health*'s Best Book of the Year Award for 2002 under the category of Hope).

Dr. Jones has given inspiring yet practical presentations to a wide variety of audiences, including colleges and universities, businesses, churches, sustainability symposiums, service conferences and global citizenship summits.

He has been interviewed for radio and television in both the US and Canada and was featured in the documentary film *50 Ways To Save The Planet*. In 2005, his work inspired the creation of The Better World Handbook Festival in Vancouver, BC. He has lived, studied, and worked in many parts of Europe, Asia, and Central America.

He has won numerous awards for his work in the classroom and is currently an Assistant Professor of Sociology in the Department of Sociology & Anthropology at Holy Cross College in Worcester, MA.

If you are interested in learning more about how you can support this work or would like to schedule a speaking engagement, please send an email to:

doctorjones@betterworldshopper.org

NOTES

NOTES

ABOUT NEW SOCIETY PUBLISHERS

New Society Publishers is an activist, solutions-oriented publisher focused on publishing books for a world of change. Our books offer tips, tools, and insights from leading experts in sustainable building, homesteading, climate change, environment, conscientious commerce, renewable energy, and more—positive solutions for troubled times.

We're proud to hold to the highest environmental and social standards of any publisher in North America. This is why some of our books might cost a little more. We think it's worth it!

DON'T EAT THIS BOOK *(but you could)*

- We print all our books in North America, never overseas
- All our books are printed on 100% **post-consumer recycled paper**, processed chlorine-free, with low-VOC vegetable-based inks (since 2002)
- Our corporate structure is an innovative employee shareholder agreement, so we're one-third employee-owned (since 2015)
- We're carbon-neutral (since 2006)
- We're certified as a B Corporation (since 2016)

At New Society Publishers, we care deeply about *what* we publish—but also about *how* we do business.

New Society Publishers
ENVIRONMENTAL BENEFITS STATEMENT

For every 5,000 books printed, New Society saves the following resources:[1]

9	Trees
815	Pounds of Solid Waste
896	Gallons of Water
1,169	Kilowatt Hours of Electricity
1,481	Pounds of Greenhouse Gases
6	Pounds of HAPs, VOCs, and AOX Combined
2	Cubic Yards of Landfill Space

[1] Environmental benefits are calculated based on research done by the Environmental Defense Fund and other members of the Paper Task Force who study the environmental impacts of the paper industry.

Certified B Corporation

FSC www.fsc.org MIX Paper from responsible sources FSC® C016245

new society PUBLISHERS www.newsociety.com